M000122089

Idioms
and Other English Expressions

Developed by
Timothy Rasinski

a bird's eye view

Authors

Kathleen Knoblock and Kathleen N. Kopp

SHELL EDUCATION

Credits

Editor
Lisa Greathouse

Assistant Editor
Leslie Huber, M.A.

Editorial Director
Dona Herweck Rice

Editor-in-Chief
Sharon Coan, M.S.Ed.

Editorial Manager
Gisela Lee, M.A.

Creative Director
Lee Aucoin

Illustration Manager
Timothy J. Bradley

Interior Layout Design
Robin Erickson

Publisher
Corinne Burton, M.A.Ed

Shell Education
5301 Oceanus Drive
Huntington Beach, CA 92649-1030
http://www.shelleducation.com
ISBN 978-1-4258-0159-5
© 2008 Shell Educational Publishing, Inc.
Reprinted 2013

The classroom teacher may reproduce copies of materials in this book for classroom use only. The reproduction of any part for an entire school or school system is strictly prohibited. No part of this publication may be transmitted, stored, or recorded in any form without written permission from the publisher.

Table of Contents

The No Child Left Behind (NCLB) legislation mandates that all states adopt academic standards that identify the skills students will learn in kindergarten through grade 12. While many states had already adopted academic standards prior to NCLB, the legislation set requirements to ensure the standards were detailed and comprehensive.

Standards are designed to focus instruction and guide adoption of curricula. Standards are statements that describe the criteria necessary for students to meet specific academic goals. They define the knowledge, skills, and content students should acquire at each level. Standards are also used to develop standardized tests to evaluate students' academic progress.

In many states today, teachers are required to demonstrate how their lessons meet state standards. State standards are used in the development of Shell Education products, so educators can be assured that they meet the academic requirements of each state.

How to Find Your State Correlations

Shell Education is committed to producing educational materials that are research- and standards-based. In this effort, all products are correlated to the academic standards of the 50 states, the District of Columbia, and the Department of Defense Dependent Schools. A correlation report customized for your state can be printed directly from the following website: **http://www.shelleducation.com**. If you require assistance in printing correlation reports, please contact Customer Service at 1-877-777-3450.

McREL Compendium

Shell Education uses the Mid-continent Research for Education and Learning (McREL) Compendium to create standards correlations. Each year, McREL analyzes state standards and revises the compendium. By following this procedure, they are able to produce a general compilation of national standards.

All of the following McREL standards apply to each lesson in this book.

McREL Standard, Level, and Benchmark	Standard
Reading 5.I.1	The student uses mental images based on pictures and print to aid in comprehension of text.
Reading 5.I.6	The student understands level-appropriate sight words and reading vocabulary.
Reading 5.I.8	The student reads aloud familiar stories, poems, and passages with fluency and expression (e.g., rhythm, flow, meter, tempo, pitch, tone, intonation).
Reading 5.II.1	The student previews text (e.g., skims material; uses pictures, textual clues, and text format).
Reading 5.II.3	The student makes, confirms, and revises simple predictions about what will be found in a text (e.g., uses prior knowledge and ideas presented in text, illustrations, titles, topic sentences, key words, and foreshadowing clues).
Reading 5.II.6	The student uses word reference materials to determine the meaning, pronunciation, and derivations of unknown words.
Reading 6.II.7	The student understands the ways in which language is used in literary texts (e.g., personification, alliteration, onomatopoeia, simile, metaphor, imagery, hyperbole, rhythm).
Writing 1.I.8	The student writes for different purposes (e.g., to entertain, inform, learn, communicate ideas).
Writing 1.II.2	The student uses strategies to draft and revise written work.

The National Reading Panel (2000) has identified vocabulary as an essential component of effective literacy instruction. When students don't know the meanings of the words and phrases in the texts they read, they are likely to experience difficulty in sufficiently understanding those very same texts.

Some of the most difficult vocabulary to understand are those words and phrases that don't reflect their literal meanings—idioms. Idioms are words that are essentially metaphorical in nature (Harris & Hodges, 1995; Riccio, 1980). When a person writes "It's raining cats and dogs," he or she does not mean that dogs and cats are literally falling out of the sky, but that it is raining hard. When another writes "Birds of a feather…" he or she is referring most likely to a group of people with common interests or characteristics and not animals that fly.

Idioms and figurative language are part and parcel of oral and written language. English is rich in idioms (Harris & Hodges, 1995). Petrosky (1980) estimates that adults may use over a half million figures of speech over the course of a year.

Because English is so filled with idioms, it can be difficult to understand (Blachowicz & Fisher, 2002) and translate into another language (Harris & Hodges, 1995). All of us at one time or another have come across a figure of speech that we don't understand because we have not been previously exposed to it and were not told the meaning of the phrase or given sufficient clues to make sense of it. Children, by their very nature of having limited life experiences, are more likely to encounter figurative language that they do not understand. This is especially true of English language learners who have had even less exposure to experiences involving the English language.

The use of idioms and other forms of figurative language in writing is a characteristic of high-quality literature (Blachowicz & Fisher, 2002). Authors include idioms in their writing to clarify their messages and make their messages more interesting for readers. "Figurative language uses comparisons, contrasts, and unusual juxtapositions of words to draw our attention to aspects of the world we live in" (Blachowicz & Fisher, 2002, p. 79). However, if a reader is unfamiliar with the idioms in the text, he or she is likely to have a poor or limited understanding of the text.

Thus, the study of idioms is certainly worthwhile, as great awareness and understanding of idiomatic language can enhance students' understanding of the texts they are asked to read. Yet most core reading programs do not provide sufficient instructional coverage on idioms and other forms of figurative language. Thus, I have developed this vocabulary program as a means to provide specific and engaging instruction on idiomatic language for students. As students become more acquainted with idioms, reading comprehension will improve.

The major intent of *Idioms and Other English Expressions*, then, is to improve students' reading comprehension and overall reading achievement. However, as noted above, high-quality writing is marked by the use of idioms and other forms of figurative language. Thus, students' writing is a second beneficiary of use of this instructional program. As students' knowledge and use of idiomatic language improves, the quality of their writing will likely show measurable gains as well.

I hope that you and your students will find *Idioms and Other English Expressions* engaging and enjoyable as well as effective in improving reading and writing. The program was designed to make word study fun for students. So when it comes to teaching vocabulary, don't sit on the fence, don't have cold feet, and don't try to pull any strings. Let me do the honors and make heads and tails out of teaching idiomatic vocabulary for your students. Before you know it, you'll be standing on your own two feet, teaching idioms will be as comfortable as an old shoe, and your students will be head over heels in love with idioms for reading and writing.

Best wishes,

Timothy Rasinski

References and Resources

Blachowicz, C., and P. Fisher. 2002. *Teaching vocabulary in all classrooms.* 2nd ed. Columbus: Merrill/Prentice-Hall.

Fry, E. 2002. *The vocabulary teacher's book of lists.* San Francisco: Jossey-Bass.

Fry, E., and J. Kress. 2006. *The reading teacher's book of lists.* San Francisco: Jossey-Bass.

Harris, T. L. and R. E. Hodges, eds. 1995. *The literacy dictionary: The vocabulary of reading and writing.* Newark, DE: International Reading Association.

Johnson, D. D. 2001. *Vocabulary in the elementary and middle school.* Boston: Allyn & Bacon.

National Reading Panel. 2000. *The report of the National Reading Panel.* Washington, DC: U.S. Department of Education.

Newton, E., N. Padak, and T. Rasinski. 2007. *Evidence-based instruction in reading: A professional development guide to vocabulary (Evidence-Based Instruction in Reading).* Boston: Allyn & Bacon.

Petrosky, A. R. 1980. *The inferences we make: Children and literature. Language Arts 57:* 149–156.

Riccio, O. M. 1980. *The intimate art of writing poetry.* Englewood Cliffs, NJ: Prentice-Hall.

Idioms and other expressions can be confusing to native English speakers. They can be especially challenging for students who are English language learners. Here are a few ideas you can use with students who would benefit from scaffolding activities to help them comprehend nonliteral expressions.

Make Connections with Oral Language Experience

Have students work collaboratively to share situations that most students have experienced, and embellish them with creative language. The list below provides a few situations. Present one situation and complete it as a model. Example: Once I ate so much that I felt like _____ (a stuffed pig; I'd eaten an elephant; a giant meatball . . .). Then ask students to think of other ways to complete the statement; the more outrageous, the better! Allow students time to work in pairs to complete the statements below (or they may think of some on their own), and share them with the class. Have the pairs record their favorite expressions on a sentence strip. Post them on a bulletin board entitled, "Our Class Has Gone 'Hog Wild' Over Idioms!"

1. I remember a time that I was as scared as . . .
2. My family reminds me of . . .
3. I remember a time that I was as mad as . . .
4. Once I tried a food that was more disgusting than . . .
5. It once rained so hard, I thought . . .

Preteach Each Unit's Expressions

Students who need additional time to learn new skills and concepts benefit from pre-teaching activities. Meet with small groups of students who may need this additional instruction prior to teaching the unit to the whole class. Introduce each expression and discuss its meaning, preferably with pictures or illustrations, or by drawing on students' prior experiences.

Substitute Literal for Figurative

Since figurative language is abstract, help students better understand the meanings of expressions by substituting the literal meanings for the figurative when reading the How It Is Used sample sentences in each unit. Model this for students during the first two units, and then have students work in groups of three or four for the remaining units. Ask one group to reread their literal statements for the class. Compare how this group's statements differ from others, and why this may be so.

Flash Cards

Assign each pair of students a different idiom to define (10 groups in all, one for each from the Ten to Teach list in each unit). Use 5-inch by 8-inch note cards, one per idiom. Students write the expression on one side, and the meaning on the back. They show the expression to their partners and their partners say the meaning. For an added challenge, the person being quizzed uses the idiom correctly in a sentence. Place the cards at a literacy center for students to use to practice either during center time or when they have free time.

Each unit plan presents 20 idioms connected to a single theme: 10 idioms are instructed directly; 10 additional idioms are included under *More to Mention*. The following activities have reproducible student pages, which may be used to extend or supplement the unit plans.

Idioms in the News

A news article titled "Volcano Erupts" may grab some readers' attention, but one that reads "Mount Flash Blows Its Top" will surely entice more readers. With this activity, students use idioms to create interesting headlines to catch readers' attention for suggested story lines (reproducible page 9). Another idea is to have students read a current newspaper article of interest and rewrite it and its headline using idioms.

Hot Deals

Students use idioms as an advertising ploy to capture consumers' attention for a product or service of their choice (reproducible page 10). Encourage students to peruse local advertisements for the use of idioms or revise an advertisement using idioms. Post students' original posters in the hallway or around the building.

Once Upon a Blue Moon

Students are provided a set of characters, settings, and situations (conflicts) for which they write the beginning of a story using an idiom (reproducible page 11). Their beginnings may be one sentence or several. Following completion of the page, have students place their work in their writing folders to use during writer's workshop when they are "stuck" getting started on a new piece of writing.

A Reader's and Writer's Idiom Thesaurus

These two reproducible pages (12 and 13) suggest several idioms and expressions for commonly used words. Students may keep these pages in their writing folders for reference during creative writing. Help students embellish their writing by referring to and using the idioms instead of more simple vocabulary. Encourage students to add to the thesaurus on their own papers when they find an idiom they like. Each time a student uses one of the idioms, acknowledge its use.

Idioms and Other Expressions: A Reference List for Readers and Writers

These four reproducible pages (14–17) list the idioms and expressions, both in the *Ten to Teach* and in the *More to Mention* columns in the unit plans. Students may keep a copy of these pages in their writing folders, or the pages may be placed at a writing center to use when students are drafting or revising a piece of written work.

Name _____ Date _____

Idioms in the News

When deciding on a news article to read, the first attention grabber is the headline. A news story may have a better chance of catching a person's interest if it has an interesting title. For example, the headline "Skateboarders Go Over the Edge" may lead the reader to think some skateboarders fell off a cliff. But if "Over the Edge" is used as an idiom, the article may explain how skateboarders did something wrong, or pushed their limits. The only way to find out is to read the article!

Directions: Read these story lines. Create an interesting headline that uses an idiom to catch the reader's attention.

1. Families line up a full day in advance outside a ticket office to be the first people in line to purchase concert tickets that will sell out quickly.

   Newsworthy headline: _____

2. A boy teaches his dog how to water ski.

   Newsworthy headline: _____

   _____

3. The local zoo discovers that two of its penguins have disappeared.

   Newsworthy headline: _____

4. Your school cafeteria installs a real barbecue smoker (or an ice cream parlor, or any other new and interesting food creation).

   Newsworthy headline: _____

5. A nearby playground opens a mini-rollercoaster.

   Newsworthy headline: _____

   _____

Bonus! Choose one of the headlines you just wrote, or think of one of your own. Write a news story for the headline. Use at least three additional idioms or expressions in the news story.

Name _____ Date _____

Hot Deals

Companies often use different tactics to advertise their products and services. They may use celebrity endorsements, offer new and interesting product lines, or appeal to a person's senses, perhaps by promoting a food's health benefits. The use of idioms can be another way companies catch a potential buyer's attention. Once they have your attention, they hope you'll buy their product or service.

Directions: Plan and create an advertisement poster for a product or service of your choice. Use at least three idioms to grab a buyer's attention. Use this page to plan your poster. Then create your poster on poster paper or a plain sheet of paper.

1. Choose a product or service to advertise. Here are some examples:

   Personal-care products (shampoo, lotion, etc.)   Sports event, concert

   Sports equipment (skateboard, weights, etc.)   Salon services (haircuts, etc.)

   Clothing   Bicycle repair

   Food   Electronic repair

   Electronic toy or gadget

2. List at least five idioms related to the product or service you chose.
   Example: Pet grooming (service)
   Don't go to the dogs.
   Make your pooch pretty as a picture.
   At Pooch Parlor, we don't horse around.
   Perk up those dog days of summer.
   We don't cut corners at Kitty Corner.

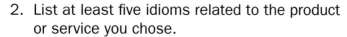

_____

_____

_____

_____

3. Circle the three idioms you will use in your poster.

4. Use the back of this page to sketch your poster.

5. Design and create an advertising poster that includes the three idioms you circled above. Use color and visuals (pictures, starbursts, or block letters, for example) to get the consumer's attention. Your poster should clearly identify the name of the product or service and include eye-catching displays and words to attract attention.

Name _____ Date _____

Once Upon a Blue Moon

If a story doesn't grab your interest within the first few pages, you may be inclined to set it aside and not read it. Great story beginnings can motivate readers to continue reading.

Directions: Write an attention-grabbing story beginning for each of the three story lines below. Use at least one idiom in the story's beginning. Write your beginnings on the back of this page or use additional paper, if needed. Remember to just write the beginning of the story.

Example: Henry was *beside himself* with excitement to check the kittens in the box beneath his bed when he woke in the morning. Jubilee had just given birth to six of the cutest kittens he had ever seen. But when he lifted his bedspread and peeked underneath his bed, Henry could have been *knocked over with a feather* to find only four kittens nestled beside the exhausted Jubilee!

Story 1:

Characters: Uncle Ed and Aunt Beatrice

Setting: At a farm

Situation: Uncle Ed's prized pig escaped his pen and is racing all over Aunt Beatrice's kitchen while she tries to get breakfast ready.

Story beginning: _____

_____

_____

Story 2:

Characters: You and your friend _____

Setting: At the movies

Situation: The popcorn maker overloads, and popcorn explodes all over the lobby.

Story beginning: _____

_____

_____

Story 3:

Characters: A younger brother or sister

Setting: At home

Situation: Your younger brother or sister was playing with a wrench and took apart your bike.

Story beginning: _____

_____

_____

Name _____ Date _____

A Reader's and Writer's Idiom Thesaurus

A thesaurus is a book that lists words related to one another in meaning, usually giving synonyms and antonyms. What is another way to say *look for*? If you look in a thesaurus, you might find: *search*, *hunt*, and *investigate*. These words are fine, but you could also describe *look for* as an idiom. You could *poke around*, *dig something up*, or *hunt high and low*. You may even *leave no stone unturned*.

The following bold words are general words. Beside each word is a list of synonyms as well as a list of idioms or other expressions that mean the same or almost the same thing in a more colorful way. This can be your personal idiom thesaurus when you are reading or writing.

Word	Word Synonyms	Idiom Synonyms
cute	adorable, attractive, pretty, precious, sweet	cute as a bug's ear, cute as a button, a pretty sight
eat	chew, consume, devour, feast, munch	have a bite to eat, chow down, feeding frenzy, gobble up
excited	delighted, elated, enthusiastic, happy	beside oneself, charged up, chomping at the bit, gung-ho
fast	hurried, quick, speedy	fast and furious, in a New York minute, pedal to the metal, fast as lightning
good	decent, nice, perfect, pleasant, suitable	crackerjack, doozy, over the top, top drawer

On My Own

Directions: Insert your own general word, a list of synonyms, and at least two idiom synonyms for it.

Word: _____

Word Synonyms: _____

Idiom Synonyms: _____

Name _____ Date _____

A Reader's and Writer's Idiom Thesaurus (cont.)

Word	Word Synonyms	Idiom Synonyms
happy	content, pleased, satisfied	happy as a clam, happy-go-lucky, pleased as punch
hurry	accelerate, hasten, quicken	get a move on, quick as a wink, shake a leg, step on it
laugh	chuckle, giggle, snicker	belly laugh, bust a gut, split your sides
mad	angry, frustrated, infuriated	loose cannon, mad as a hatter
run	dash, race, sprint	cut and run, fly like the wind, run for it
say	blurt, declare, proclaim, speak	pipe up, speak your mind, tell it like it is
trouble	concern, distress, worry	in a fix, caught with your pants down, in a pickle
try	attempt, strive, undertake	go out on a limb, go the extra mile, try your luck
worried	anxious, jumpy, nervous, tense	on edge, on pins and needles, tied up in knots
wow	exemplary, great, terrific	Eureka!, something to shout about, the greatest thing since sliced bread

On My Own

Directions: Insert your own general word, a list of synonyms, and at least two idiom synonyms for it.

Word: _____

Word Synonyms: _____

Idiom Synonyms: _____

Idioms and Other Expressions: A Reference List for Readers and Writers

Idioms About Animals

dog-eat-dog

straight from the horse's mouth

the cat's meow

squirrel away

monkey around

hoof it

whole hog

all bark and no bite

horse of a different color

goose is cooked

take the bull by the horns

play cat and mouse

eat crow

bark up the wrong tree

cry wolf

chomping at the bit

hit the bull's eye

get one's goat

have goose bumps

bird's-eye view

cry crocodile tears

Idioms Using Numbers

(go) fifty-fifty

think twice

no two ways about it

nickel and dime

one step ahead

on all fours

take forty winks

put in one's two cents

wouldn't touch it with a ten-foot pole

two left feet

baker's dozen

have one up on someone

two faced

the third degree

at the eleventh hour

back to square one

give me five

a dime a dozen

take five

four corners of the earth

put two and two together

Idioms About Body Parts

get off on the wrong foot

nose out of joint

a tongue-lashing

shake a leg

breathing down one's neck

fight tooth and nail

the cold shoulder

a pain in the neck

get out of hand

don't have a leg to stand on

do an about-face

word of mouth

slip of the tongue

in over one's head

in one ear and out the other

lend me an ear

chilled to the bone

bite one's lip

fall flat on one's face

put one's foot in one's mouth

Idioms and Other Expressions:
A Reference List for Readers and Writers *(cont.)*

Idioms With Heart

with a heavy heart	heartbroken	have a heart
heart stood still	heart and soul	in a heartbeat
heart of gold	place in one's heart	change of heart
from the heart	take heart	heart of stone
heart set on	lose heart	know by heart
heart in the right place	heart-to-heart	
didn't have the heart	follow one's heart	

Idioms With Feeling

wake up on the wrong side of the bed	flip one's lid	down in the dumps
rub someone the wrong way	for the birds	at the end of one's rope
on cloud nine	bent out of shape	got the short end of the stick
in the hot seat	walking on air	have an ax to grind
run into a brick wall	blow a fuse	between a rock and a hard place
go out on a limb	bored stiff	up against the wall

Water and Weather Idioms

under the weather	a flood of tears	an icy stare
raining cats and dogs	burning up (with fever)	all steamed up
soaked to the bone	in hot water	turn on the waterworks
usual sunny self	sky-high temperature	on the sunny side of the street
like water off a duck's back	a wet blanket	rain on someone's parade
in a fog	wash away the tears	as fresh as springtime
misty-eyed	a snow job	

Idioms and Other Expressions:
A Reference List for Readers and Writers (cont.)

Idioms About Objects

piece of cake	hats off	bark up the wrong tree
hit the hay	in the bag	on the fence
in the driver's seat	couch potato	be a fly on the wall
the short end of the stick	humble pie	walk on eggs
leave in the dust	ham it up	
hands down	in the same boat	
second fiddle	flew the coop	

Expressions That Are Similes

as different as night and day	feel/look like a million bucks	like a fish out of water
like a bump on a log	as stubborn as a mule	as cute as a button
as hungry as a bear	like a hog	as solid as a rock
eats like a horse	as snug as a bug in a rug	(run) like the wind
as strong as an ox	as sick as a dog	as wise as an owl
as sweet as honey	as gentle as a lamb	
eats like a bird	as cool as a cucumber	

Expressions That Are Metaphors

top dog	time stood still	at the end of one's rope
make a beeline	all bark and no bite	stretch the point
eager beaver	all pumped up	break the silence
round up (everyone)	caught one's breath	hit a snag
chew on something	see the writing on the wall	hard to swallow
puff up	steamed up	on the edge of one's seat
buy into it	left holding the bag	the icing on the cake
keep one's paws off	take forty winks	

Idioms and Other Expressions:
A Reference List for Readers and Writers (cont.)

Expressions That Exaggerate (Hyperbole)

go through the roof

head over heels

cost an arm and a leg

until the cows come home

born yesterday

highway robbery

everything but the kitchen sink

find a needle in a haystack

made of money

on top of the world

when pigs fly

burns me up

ton of money

on one's last leg

over my dead body

the sky's the limit

bursting at the seams

turn over in one's grave

chilled to the bone

die of boredom

full of hot air

the last straw

Common Sayings (Proverbs)

That's easier said than done.

If the shoe fits, wear it.

Birds of a feather flock together.

Blood is thicker than water.

Don't look a gift horse in the mouth.

Be careful what you wish for.

A stitch in time saves nine.

You can't teach an old dog new tricks.

Don't put all your eggs in one basket.

Time flies when you're having fun.

Necessity is the mother of invention.

Let sleeping dogs lie.

Haste makes waste.

Too many cooks spoil the broth.

Strike while the iron is hot.

Variety is the spice of life.

Cat got your tongue?

Two wrongs don't make a right.

No news is good news.

Idioms About Animals

This unit highlights idioms related to animals. Below are two lists of idioms that focus on animals. The first, *Ten to Teach*, presents the 10 expressions introduced and taught in this unit. The second, *More to Mention*, offers additional expressions in this theme that you may want to mention or use to create additional activities.

Ten to Teach

1. straight from the horse's mouth
2. the cat's meow
3. squirrel away
4. monkey around
5. hoof it

6. all bark and no bite
7. goose is cooked
8. take the bull by the horns
9. play cat and mouse
10. bark up the wrong tree

More to Mention

▶ dog-eat-dog*
▶ horse of a different color*
▶ eat crow*
▶ cry wolf

▶ whole hog
▶ chomping at the bit
▶ hit the bull's-eye
▶ get one's goat

▶ have goose bumps
▶ bird's-eye view
▶ cry crocodile tears

*These idioms are also included in the story but are not highlighted individually in the unit.

Using This Unit

Begin by reading to students the basic *Ten to Teach* idioms. First, ask students if they have ever heard or used any of these expressions, and if so, how and where. Next, read the expressions again, and this time ask the students to listen for anything they have in common. Be sure they see that all the expressions refer to animals. Teach or review the definition of an *idiom*—an expression that means something other than what the words actually say. If you like, read the list a third time and let students speculate on what each idiom might really mean.

On the next page is a story that includes the *Ten to Teach* idioms (along with three *More to Mention* idioms). Note that the story is not intended to be an example of good writing; it would not be natural to use 13 idioms in such a short piece. The purpose of the story is simply to use all the expressions in context. The story is at approximately a 3.4 reading level. Use this information to read it aloud to students, have them read it, or both. This reproducible page includes the story and questions for students to answer related to the idioms used.

The final five pages of the unit introduce the basic *Ten to Teach* idioms individually, two to a page. These can be reproduced and used as is, or cut apart into separate cards. Use these after the story to reinforce the meanings of the idioms or to test students' understanding of them. Or, use them before the story as preparation for reading or for scaffolding as needed.

Optional: Use one of the ideas or activities in the introductory section of this book as an extension or follow-up to the unit.

Name _____ Date _____

Below is a story that includes 13 idioms about animals. Can you tell what they mean?

Case Closed

I've been a police detective for 25 years, and in this **dog-eat-dog** world, I thought I had seen it all. Coming from anyone else, you might not believe this story. However, I am going to give it to you **straight from the horse's mouth.**

A couple of years ago, a man had a pet that he thought was **the cat's meow**. It wasn't a cat, though. It wasn't even a dog. It was an alligator. At first he thought it was cool. It was just a baby and only a foot or so long. He kept it **squirreled away** in his backyard. Then, when people would come over, he'd **monkey around** with it and they would **hoof it** out of there. He'd just laugh because Alley was **all bark and no bite**.

But, as time passed, Alley grew. Soon he was more than six feet long. Now that's a **horse of a different color**. The man came to realize that if the police found out that he had Alley, his **goose would be cooked**. It was time to **take the bull by the horns**.

Late one night, the man and his buddy wrapped Alley in a blanket and carried him to the edge of a lake in a nearby neighborhood park and set him loose. They thought he would never be seen again, but he was—and by a lot of people. For a while, Alley seemed to **play cat and mouse** with the officials to avoid being captured. That's where I come in. I didn't catch Alley, but I did catch the guy who put him there. Believe me, when I got to the bottom of this, that guy had to **eat crow**. He was **barking up the wrong tree** with me!

It took a while, but both the criminal and Alley were caught, and both are behind bars—one in jail and the other at the zoo!

Read or listen to the story again. Then answer these questions about the idioms. To help you find them, the idioms are in **dark print** in the story.

1. At first, did the man think his pet was loud and frightening or wonderful?

    _____

2. Which idiom explains that the man took charge of his growing gator?

    _____

3. According to the man, was Alley fierce or friendly?

    _____

4. Would you have **hoofed it** along with the other visitors? Explain.

    _____

5. Would you **monkey around** with an alligator? Explain.

    _____

Name _____ Date _____

Idiom ▶ **straight from the horse's mouth**

Meaning ▶ information directly from the source, not from someone else

How It Is Used ▶ My brother told me that our parents were going to take us to King's Amusement Park next weekend, but I didn't believe him. I decided to ask my dad, so I'd hear it *straight from the horse's mouth*.

Which Is Right? ▶ Read the two selections. Choose the one in which *straight from the horse's mouth* is used as an idiom. Circle the number of your choice.

❶ Paul had just shown Polly how to put a bridle on his horse, Fawn. When Polly went to remove the bridle, she pulled it *straight from the horse's mouth*.

❷ There were rumors that we would be having a class party on Friday. I asked our teacher so that I'd hear it *straight from the horse's mouth*.

Idiom ▶ **the cat's meow**

Meaning ▶ really great

How It Is Used ▶ Gina had always liked bejeweled clothes and shiny jewelry. When she spotted a pair of jeans with gold, blue, and green gems, she exclaimed, "Those jeans are *the cat's meow*!"

Which Is Right? ▶ Read the two selections. Choose the one in which *the cat's meow* is used as an idiom. Circle the number of your choice.

❶ As they left the theater, Jenna and Anne talked excitedly about the great scenes in the movie they had just seen. Anne told Jenna that her favorite part was the big musical number at the end. Jenna agreed: "That scene was *the cat's meow*," she said.

❷ Hilary had one important job when she watched her neighbor's house. When she heard *the cat's meow*, she knew to let him in for food and water.

Name _____   Date _____

Idiom ▶ **squirrel away**

Meaning ▶ hide things or put them away for a later time

How It Is Used ▶ Fran couldn't help but notice that her good markers kept disappearing. She spied on her little sister, Agnes, as Agnes snuck into her room, took two markers, and then *squirreled them away* in her own art box.

Which Is Right? ▶ Read the two selections. Choose the one in which *squirrel away* is used as an idiom. Circle the number of your choice.

❶ Peter kept asking his mom for pennies. He placed them in a sock, and hid them in the back of his drawer. When Peter's mom was putting his clothes away, she discovered his bundle of pennies. She figured that he must be *squirreling them away* to save up for a new toy.

❷ Hugh's stuffed animals were all over his bedroom floor. He had nearly finished putting them all back, when he heard his mom call from the living room, "Hugh! Come put this *squirrel away!*"

Idiom ▶ **monkey around**

Meaning ▶ fool around; goof off; play instead of work

How It Is Used ▶ Freddie and his friends were splashing and squirting one another in the pool. His sister Terry and her friends did not want to get wet. They asked the boys to stop *monkeying around*.

Which Is Right ▶ Read the two selections. Choose the one in which *monkey around* is used as an idiom. Circle the number of your choice.

❶ Bonnie and her mom loved the zoo. When they entered the primates area, they found themselves surrounded by apes, chimps, and lemurs. Bonnie pointed out a feisty *monkey around* the banana tree. He called and screeched until Bonnie threw a peanut for him.

❷ Jake and his friends were enjoying their time on the beach. Before long, they were kicking sand and tossing one another into the water. The lifeguard blew his whistle and instructed them to stop *monkeying around*. If they didn't, they would be asked to leave the beach.

Idioms About Animals (cont.)

Name _____ Date _____

Idiom ▶ **hoof it**

Meaning ▶ move quickly; get away fast

How It Is Used ▶ Della and Vera came across a hole in the ground in the woods. Rather than leave it alone, they poked a stick in it to see how deep it was. When a snake emerged, they *hoofed it* down the forest path.

Which Is Right? ▶ Read the two selections. Choose the one in which *hoof it* is used as an idiom. Circle the number of your choice.

❶ The riding lessons were a lot of fun. Part of the lesson included looking over the horses to be sure they were ready for riding. If Delores hadn't noticed her horse's *hoof, it* may have injured itself along the trail.

❷ Carlos discovered he was falling behind his classmates on the field trip to the museum. Rather than be left behind, he *hoofed it* to catch up.

Idiom ▶ **all bark and no bite**

Meaning ▶ something that seems vicious or ferocious, but is really harmless or kind

How It Is Used ▶ Lyle didn't like going to his friend Jacob's house when Jacob's big brother was there. His brother always seemed so mean. But when Lyle spent the weekend at Jacob's house, he realized that Jacob's brother was *all bark and no bite*.

Which Is Right? ▶ Read the two selections. Choose the one in which *all bark and no bite* is used as an idiom. Circle the number of your choice.

❶ Sam was not sure whether to trust the new class pet, a foot-long snake. It looked so scary and hissed. But when Sam was chosen to care for it for the week, he realized that the snake was *all bark and no bite*.

❷ My three-year-old sister had always been afraid of our neighbor's dogs. They were always barking and waking her up. But when she got to know them, she realized they were friendly. "These dogs *all bark and no bite*," she said in baby talk.

Name _____ Date _____

Idiom ▶ **goose is cooked**

Meaning ▶ in trouble; caught doing something wrong

How It Is Used ▶ Rose was sure she could sneak in her late research paper to Mr. Farley without getting caught. She simply shoved it in a stack when no one was looking. The next day, when Mr. Farley called Rose over to his desk, she knew her *goose was cooked*!

Which Is Right? ▶ Read the two selections. Choose the one in which *goose is cooked* is used as an idiom. Circle the number of your choice.

❶ Aunt Mae had a wonderful meal planned for the family get-together. All she told us was that the main dish was a surprise. Finally, it was time to eat! Aunt Mae called for Uncle Harold to get ready to carve because the *goose was cooked*.

❷ Brian had promised he would keep the family's new puppy out of trouble while his parents were away. While Brian was playing video games, the puppy was busy chewing on shoes and gnawing on furniture! Brian did his best to hide the evidence, but when his parents opened the door, he was still holding a nibbled shoe. Brian knew right then that his *goose was cooked*.

Idiom ▶ **take the bull by the horns**

Meaning ▶ take charge; face or confront a difficult task

How It Is Used ▶ Our principal, Mrs. Schultz, raced into the cafeteria to put a stop to the food fight. When she demanded that those responsible for starting it step forward, no one spoke. She threatened to expel every student who threw food. Later, Chris, who had thrown the first wad of mashed potatoes, decided to *take the bull by the horns* and admit he started it.

Which Is Right? ▶ Read the two selections. Choose the one in which *take the bull by the horns* is used as an idiom. Circle the number of your choice.

❶ No one in Jeffrey's class wanted to be the first one to present his or her report. Jeffrey decided to *take the bull by the horns* and volunteer to go first.

❷ Joseph wanted to see a real bullfight while his family was on vacation in Spain. He thought it was interesting how the handlers *take the bull by the horns*.

Name _____ Date _____

Idiom ▶ **play cat and mouse**

Meaning ▶ try to trick someone so you can catch or escape from him or her; try to find someone or something that is hiding from you

How It Is Used ▶ Squirrels were always trying to steal the birds' food. They seemed to *play cat and mouse* with Mr. Gerard, who refilled his bird feeder every day. Finally, Mr. Gerard rigged his bird feeder so the squirrels could no longer get to the food.

Which Is Right? ▶ Read the two selections. Choose the one in which *play cat and mouse* is used as an idiom. Circle the number of your choice.

❶ After months of *playing cat and mouse* with a local bank robber, the police tracked him down and put him behind bars.

❷ My grandma bought my brother a set of animal masks. He and his friend Bobby put on a show, pretending they were different animals. They especially liked *playing cat and mouse.*

Idiom ▶ **bark up the wrong tree**

Meaning ▶ look in the wrong place; ask the wrong person; answer a question incorrectly

How It Is Used ▶ Kyle went to his mom to ask where he left his shoes. His mom replied, "I don't keep track of your clothes. I have no idea where you left them. You are *barking up the wrong tree.*"

Which Is Right? ▶ Read the two selections. Choose the one in which *barking up the wrong tree* is used as an idiom. Circle the number of your choice.

❶ Mark's cat climbed up the tree outside his house. Minutes later, his beagle ran outside and started barking in front of the neighbor's tree. How strange, Mark thought, for his dog to be *barking up the wrong tree*!

❷ When Mrs. Moss asked Jane to locate Washington state on a map, Jane pointed to Washington, D.C. "That's the wrong side of the country," said Mrs. Moss. "You are *barking up the wrong tree.*"

Idioms Using Numbers

This unit highlights idioms that use numbers. Below are two lists of idioms that focus on numbers. The first, *Ten to Teach*, presents the 10 expressions introduced and taught in this unit. The second, *More to Mention*, offers additional expressions in this theme that you may want to mention or use to create additional activities.

Ten to Teach

1. **(go) fifty-fifty**
2. **think twice**
3. **no two ways about it**
4. **nickel and dime**
5. **put two and two together**

6. **one step ahead**
7. **on all fours**
8. **forty winks**
9. **put in one's two cents**
10. **touch (it) with a ten-foot pole**

More to Mention

▶ two left feet
▶ baker's dozen
▶ have one up on someone
▶ two faced

▶ the third degree
▶ at the eleventh hour
▶ back to square one
▶ give me five

▶ a dime a dozen
▶ take five
▶ four corners of the earth

Using This Unit

Begin by reading to students the basic *Ten to Teach* idioms. First, ask students if they have ever heard or used any of these expressions, and if so, how and where. Next, tell the students that you are going to read the expressions again, and this time they are to listen for anything they have in common. Accept all answers, and then point out that all the expressions have something to do with numbers. Teach or review the definition of an *idiom*—an expression that means something other than what the words actually say. If you like, read the list a third time and let students speculate on what each idiom might really mean.

On the next page is a story that includes the *Ten to Teach* idioms. Note that the story is not intended to be an example of good writing; it would not be natural to use 10 idioms in such a short piece. The purpose of the story is simply to use all the expressions in context. The story is at approximately a 4.0 reading level. Use this information to read it aloud to students, have them read it, or both. This reproducible page includes the story and questions for students to answer related to the idioms used.

The final five pages of the unit introduce the basic *Ten to Teach* idioms individually, two to a page. These can be reproduced and used as is, or cut apart into separate cards. Use these after the story to reinforce the meanings of the idioms or to test students' understanding of them. Or, use them before the story as preparation for reading or for scaffolding as needed.

Optional: Use one of the ideas or activities in the introductory section of this book as an extension or follow-up to the unit.

Name _____ Date _____

Below is a story that includes ten idioms using numbers. Can you tell what they mean?

Babysitting Blues

My 13-year-old sister babysits to earn extra money. One time, she agreed to watch a two-year-old and her one-year-old brother at the same time. She asked me to help. She said she would **go fifty-fifty** with me. I didn't have to **think twice** about that. **No two ways about it**—this was no **nickel and dime** job. I **put two and two together** and figured out that I could earn some serious money. How hard could it be to keep **one step ahead** of a couple of little kids?

No sooner had the parents walked out the door did I realize how wrong I was. In less than five minutes, the bigger one was screaming and the little one was crawling for the stairs. My sister tried to calm the two-year-old and I ran after the little one **on all fours**. I caught him by the diaper just before he got to the stairs.

For the next couple of hours it took both of us to keep track of these kids. I thought little kids slept a lot! These didn't even take **forty winks** the whole night. I was the one who could have used a nap!

When the parents finally arrived home, they asked how their children behaved. "Oh, just fine," said my sister. I wanted to **put in my two cents**, but I held my tongue.

On the way home, my sister turned to me and said, "Hey, you did well. Do you want to go with me on my next job?"

I was thinking that I *wouldn't* ever **touch** a babysitting job again **with a ten-foot pole**, but then she handed over half the cash and I said, "Sure. Anytime."

Read or listen to the story again. Then answer these questions about the idioms. To help you find them, the idioms are in **dark print** in the story.

1. How quickly did the two babies start causing trouble?

   _____

2. How did the writer of the story have to chase the one-year-old?

   _____

3. How did the writer feel about babysitting after they left the house? How did her feelings change after she got paid?

   _____

4. If you were the older sister, would you have split the money **fifty-fifty**? Why or why not?

   _____

Name _____   Date _____

Idiom ▶ **put two and two together**

Meaning ▶ to figure out something by using the information you have

How It Is Used ▶ I didn't know if my mom had already left, but when I saw her car was gone, I *put two and two together*.

Which Is Right? ▶ Read the two selections. Choose the one in which *put two and two together* is used as an idiom. Circle the number of your choice.

❶ Angela thought she would get 100 percent on her math exam, so she was mad when she realized that she got one problem wrong because she made a mistake just *putting two and two together*!

❷ I couldn't understand why my sister didn't want to go to the movies with her friends, but when I found out that my mom agreed to take her shopping, I *put two and two together*.

Idiom ▶ **one step ahead**

Meaning ▶ be better prepared; be more successful; make more progress than others

How It Is Used ▶ Mr. Fielding tackled one new project each weekend. This way, he felt he could stay *one step ahead* in maintaining his house.

Which Is Right? ▶ Read the two selections. Choose the one in which *one step ahead* is used as an idiom. Circle the number of your choice.

❶ The dog trainer showed the class how to walk with our dogs at our side. When our dog got *one step ahead* of us, we were supposed to tug on his leash to get him back in line.

❷ Ashley did some of next week's homework over the weekend. She wanted to stay *one step ahead* of her homework schedule so she could continue with piano lessons and soccer during the week and not fall behind in school.

Name _____ Date _____

Idiom ▶ **on all fours**

Meaning ▶ on hands and knees

How It Is Used ▶ Miss Peterson's kindergarten class visited the fire department. The students learned how to stop, drop, and roll. Then they practiced crawling *on all fours* to stay under smoke.

Which Is Right? ▶ Read the two selections. Choose the one in which *on all fours* is used as an idiom. Circle the number of your choice.

❶ Larry's mom couldn't find the family's new kitten. She even got down *on all fours* to look under the beds, tables, and chairs. Finally, the kitten sprang to freedom when she opened the pantry door.

❷ Chelsea tried to put little mittens *on all four* of her kitten's paws. But the kitten bit them off before she even took two steps.

Idiom ▶ **forty winks**

Meaning ▶ nap; sleep

How It Is Used ▶ Camp Kaleidoscope was fun, but tiring! Hilda lay on her bunk to catch *forty winks* between craft time and swimming. This way, she hoped to have enough energy to sing around the campfire long into the night.

Which Is Right? ▶ Read the two selections. Choose the one in which *forty winks* is used as an idiom. Circle the number of your choice.

❶ Gina tried to trick her sister into believing a secret code would unlock her bedroom door. "Just make *forty winks* while touching one finger to your nose. Then say 'Gina is Queen' ten times, and the door will unlock."

❷ Mr. Nester's class was on its way back from a field trip to the marina. The students were tired from a day of walking. About half the students took *forty winks* on the bus ride back to school.

Name _____ Date _____

Idiom ▶ **put in one's two cents**

Meaning ▶ include one's opinion; speak up; say something to contribute to a discussion

How It Is Used ▶ Holly thought her mom's punishment for treating her brother poorly was unfair. She knew better, though, than to *put in her two cents*, or else her mom would think she was talking back. Better to keep quiet and take the punishment.

Which Is Right? ▶ Read the two selections. Choose the one in which *put in one's two cents* is used as an idiom. Circle the number of your choice.

❶ Shelby's team was not happy about including Gale. Gale was a good enough athlete, but she would always *put in her two cents* after the team had made a decision.

❷ Pete wanted to double his chances. Instead of the usual penny, he *put in his two cents* at the wishing pond. Then he wished for a new bike for his birthday.

Idiom ▶ **touch (it) with a ten-foot pole**

Meaning ▶ not get close to something; not get involved with something; stay away from something

How It Is Used ▶ Jared's little brother likes to chase him holding lizards and frogs. Jared always runs away. Those animals are something Jared *wouldn't touch with a ten-foot pole*.

Which Is Right? ▶ Read the two selections. Choose the one in which *touch (it) with a ten-foot pole* is used as an idiom. Circle the number of your choice.

❶ When they came across what looked to be a dead raccoon, Blake and Brett ran home and grabbed an extendable pole from the garage. "You go ahead," urged Blake. "*Touch it with a ten-foot pole*. If it jumps, get ready to run."

❷ Gabrielle liked debates and giving speeches. Her friend Rachel was afraid to stand up in front of any group of people. When asked to begin their school debate, Rachel declined, telling Gabrielle, "I wouldn't *touch that job with a ten-foot pole*."

© Shell Education

Idioms about Body Parts

This unit highlights idioms about body parts. Below are two lists of idioms that focus on parts of the body. The first, *Ten to Teach*, presents the 10 expressions introduced and taught in this unit. The second, *More to Mention*, offers additional expressions in this theme that you may want to mention or use to create additional activities.

Ten to Teach

1. got off on the wrong foot
2. nose out of joint
3. a tongue-lashing
4. shake a leg
5. fight tooth and nail
6. breathing down one's neck
7. the cold shoulder
8. a pain in the neck
9. get out of hand
10. didn't have a leg to stand on

More to Mention

▶ do an about-face*
▶ in one ear and out the other*
▶ slip of the tongue
▶ in over one's head
▶ word of mouth
▶ lend me an ear
▶ chilled to the bone
▶ bite one's lip
▶ fall flat on your face
▶ put your foot in your mouth

These idioms are also included in the story but are not highlighted individually in the unit.

Using This Unit

Begin by reading to students the basic *Ten to Teach* idioms. First, ask students if they have ever heard or used any of these expressions, and if so, how and where. Next, tell the students that you are going to read the expressions again, and this time they are to listen for anything they have in common. Accept all answers, and then point out that all of the expressions have something to do with parts of the body. Teach or review the definition of an *idiom*—an expression that means something other than what the words actually say. If you like, read the list a third time and let students speculate on what each idiom might really mean.

On the next page is a story that includes the *Ten to Teach* idioms (along with two *More to Mention* idioms). Note that the story is not intended to be an example of good writing; it would not be natural to use 12 idioms in such a short piece. The purpose of the story is simply to use all the expressions in context. The story is at approximately a 4.0 reading level. Use this information to read it aloud to students, have them read it, or both. This reproducible page includes the story and questions for students to answer related to the idioms used.

The final five pages of the unit introduce the basic *Ten to Teach* idioms individually, two to a page. These can be reproduced and used as is, or cut apart into separate cards. Use these after the story to reinforce the meanings of the idioms or to test students' understanding of them. Or, use them before the story as preparation for reading or for scaffolding as needed.

Optional: Use one of the ideas or activities in the introductory section of this book as an extension or follow-up to the unit.

Name _____ Date _____

Below is a story that includes 12 idioms about body parts. Can you tell what they mean?

Museum Mayhem

Our fourth grade class went on a field trip to the Museum of Natural History. Let's just say that our trip **got off on the wrong foot**.

We were lined up waiting for the bus to pick us up. Bobby started making elephant jokes in line. Miss Feeny already had her **nose out of joint**, but we couldn't stop giggling. She made us **do an about face** and march back to the classroom. After giving us a **tongue-lashing**, she had us all line up again. The bus had already arrived, so we had to **shake a leg**.

On the bus, Bobby sat next to me. He started poking me in the ribs, and I had to **fight tooth and nail** to keep from laughing. I didn't want Miss Feeny **breathing down my neck** the whole day. I told Bobby to cut it out, but it went **in one ear and out the other**. I even tried giving him **the cold shoulder**, but he wouldn't stop being **a pain in the neck**. However, no matter what I did, Bobby kept it up, and I lost it. I started laughing, and that's when things **got out of hand**.

Miss Feeny made Bobby and me sit on the bus with Mrs. Rose while the other kids were in the museum. I guess I could've said that it was all Bobby's fault, but I knew I **didn't have a leg to stand on.**

Read or listen to the story again. Then answer these questions about the idioms. To help you find them, the idioms are in **dark print** in the story.

1. Did the field trip start off well or poorly? Explain.

   _____

2. Was Miss Feeny in a good mood or a bad mood?

   _____

3. What is one way the writer tried to keep Bobby from bothering him or her? Did it work?

   _____

4. Did the writer blame everything on Bobby? Explain.

   _____

5. Do you think both students should have been punished? Explain.

   _____

Name _____ Date _____

Idiom ▶ **got off on the wrong foot**

Meaning ▶ a bad start

How It Is Used ▶ Mom thought Jenny would make a great babysitter, but we simply *got off on the wrong foot*. As soon as the door shut behind my parents, Jenny started ordering me around, and she wouldn't let me watch what I wanted on TV. So I went to my room and slammed my bedroom door.

Which Is Right? ▶ Read the two selections. Choose the one in which *got off on the wrong foot* is used as an idiom. Circle the number of your choice.

❶ Megan was so excited to have Jill meet her friend, Sue. But the two girls *got off on the wrong foot*. Jill was insulted that Sue demanded to do all the things she wanted to do, and the girls couldn't do anything Jill or Megan wanted to do.

❷ Frank was certain he and Jeremy would win the sack race at the picnic. But when the boys began to jump, Jeremy *got off on the wrong foot*, and they both fell to the ground.

Idiom ▶ **nose out of joint**

Meaning ▶ upset; disgusted; unhappy

How It Is Used ▶ Ian felt left out when he was the last one picked for the flag football game. Rather than get his *nose out of joint*, he played hard during the game and proved his worth on the team. Next time, he wouldn't be the last pick.

Which Is Right? ▶ Read the two selections. Choose the one in which *nose out of joint* is used as an idiom. Circle the number of your choice.

❶ Marty is the first baseman on our baseball team. Last Saturday, a ball hit him in the face and afterward, it looked like his *nose was out of joint*.

❷ Mom seemed nervous when she showed Dad the mail. She hoped he wouldn't get his *nose out of joint* when he saw how much she spent on our school clothes.

Name _____ Date _____

Idiom ▶ **a tongue-lashing**

Meaning ▶ scold; speak harshly to

How It Is Used ▶ Gina knew she was in big trouble when she broke her mom's favorite lamp. She was in for a real *tongue-lashing* about respecting other people's things.

Which Is Right? ▶ Read the two selections. Choose the one in which *a tongue-lashing* is used as an idiom. Circle the number of your choice.

❶ Cindy was surprised at how spicy the Mexican food was. She felt like her mouth was on fire. Her cousin suggested she give herself *a tongue-lashing* with an ice cube to ease the pain.

❷ Jeff meant well when he took his neighbor's mail to him. When he handed over the stack of letters, he was surprised when Mr. Jones gave him *a tongue-lashing* for opening his mailbox. Jeff promised never to touch his neighbor's mail again.

Idiom ▶ **shake a leg**

Meaning ▶ move quickly; hurry up; dance

How It Is Used ▶ With Mom out of town on a business trip, George and Gary really had to *shake a leg* each morning to be ready in time for their dad to take them to school.

Which Is Right? ▶ Read the two selections. Choose the one in which *shake a leg* is used as an idiom. Circle the number of your choice.

❶ Every time we would rub the belly of our old dog, Whiskers, he would always *shake a leg*.

❷ Doris and Samantha had one more night to finish their science project for school. Since they got started late, they would really have to *shake a leg* to complete it on time.

Name _____ Date _____

Idiom ▶ **fight tooth and nail**

Meaning ▶ make a great effort to challenge or oppose someone or something; fight back hard

How It Is Used ▶ The three student council members were determined to change some things in the lunchroom. They *fought tooth and nail* to allow the sale of ice cream during lunch.

Which Is Right? ▶ Read the two selections. Choose the one in which *fight tooth and nail* is used as an idiom. Circle the number of your choice.

1 Leah's mom wanted her to get rid of some of her old toys. Leah agreed to throw out some old stuffed animals, but she *fought tooth and nail* to keep her doll collection.

2 We brought our two dogs in to the grooming shop for haircuts, but they always want to *fight tooth and nail* filings and trimmings.

Idiom ▶ **breathing down one's neck**

Meaning ▶ pay close attention to someone or his or her actions so much that it's bothersome; watch closely

How It Is Used ▶ Kyle always seemed to get into trouble in the cafeteria. The assistant principal started *breathing down his neck* in the lunchroom until Kyle began following the rules.

Which Is Right? ▶ Read the two selections. Choose the one in which *breathing down one's neck* is used as an idiom. Circle the number of your choice.

1 Joshua liked to show how his pet lizard would climb on his head and down his back. "It really tickles when he *breathes down my neck*," he says.

2 The chemicals in the science lab needed to be handled with care. Ever since Lorraine dropped a bottle of iodine, Mr. Hendrix had been *breathing down her neck* in the lab.

Name _____ Date _____

Idiom ▶ **the cold shoulder**

Meaning ▶ ignore; act unfriendly; show no interest

How It Is Used ▶ Fiona didn't understand when Amanda gave her *the cold shoulder* at school on Monday. The two girls had a great time at a sleepover party on Saturday. Perhaps Fiona did or said something at the party to upset her friend.

Which Is Right? ▶ Read the two selections. Choose the one in which *the cold shoulder* is used as an idiom. Circle the number of your choice.

❶ Mike was still upset with his older brother, James, for calling him names in front of his friends. Even though James apologized, Mike continued to give his brother *the cold shoulder*.

❷ Vera decided to bring a jacket to wear over her sleeveless dress. It might be chilly in the evening, she thought, and she didn't want to have a *cold shoulder*.

Idiom ▶ **a pain in the neck**

Meaning ▶ bothersome; annoying

How It Is Used ▶ Carl was tired when he got home from school. Having to take out the dog and feed the fish seemed like a big *pain in the neck* to him.

Which Is Right? ▶ Read the two selections. Choose the one in which *pain in the neck* is used as an idiom. Circle the number of your choice.

❶ Pedro was looking forward to spending time playing video games with his friends. He was upset to learn that his mom expected him to include his little sister in the competition. She constantly complained and whined during the games and was a complete *pain in the neck*.

❷ Mandy knew she slept with her head bent in an awkward position because when she woke up in the morning, she had a throbbing *pain in the neck*.

© Shell Education

Name _____ Date _____

Idiom ▶ **get out of hand**

Meaning ▶ not in control

How It Is Used ▶ The class enjoyed the holiday party. Things *got out of hand*, though, when Derek challenged Zack to a cupcake-eating contest. They dropped icing and crumbs all over the place!

Which Is Right? ▶ Read the two selections. Choose the one in which *get out of hand* is used as an idiom. Circle the number of your choice.

❶ Juggles the Clown was putting on a great performance at our assembly. The show *got out of hand*, however, when his water balloons exploded and splashed the audience. That was not part of the act!

❷ Ramona was excited to show her mom the ladybug she found on the leaf. When she opened her tiny fist, however, she discovered the insect had *gotten out of her hand* and escaped.

Idiom ▶ **didn't have a leg to stand on**

Meaning ▶ unsupported; without something to back up a person

How It Is Used ▶ When Rafael's mom yelled at him about leaving an empty milk jug in the refrigerator, he didn't bother to argue. With all the other times he had done this, he knew he *didn't have a leg to stand on*.

Which Is Right? ▶ Read the two selections. Choose the one in which *didn't have a leg to stand on* is used as an idiom. Circle the number of your choice.

❶ Dawn felt badly for the poor kitten in the window. It only had three legs. "How does she get up *without a leg to stand on*?" she asked the pet shop owner.

❷ Owen didn't expect the store to give him a hard time when he returned his broken watch. The warranty clearly covered the watch for all problems, so he knew the store *didn't have a leg to stand on*.

This unit highlights idioms that use the word *heart*. Below are two lists of idioms that focus on the heart. The first, *Ten to Teach*, presents the 10 expressions introduced and taught in this unit. The second, *More to Mention*, offers additional expressions in this theme that you may want to mention or use to create additional activities.

Ten to Teach

1. with a heavy heart
2. heart stood still
3. heart of gold
4. from the heart
5. heart set on

6. heart in the right place
7. didn't have the heart
8. heartbroken
9. heart and soul
10. place in one's heart

More to Mention

▶ take heart
▶ lose heart
▶ heart-to-heart

▶ follow one's heart
▶ have a heart
▶ in a heartbeat

▶ change of heart
▶ heart of stone
▶ know by heart

Using This Unit

Begin by reading to students the basic *Ten to Teach* idioms. First, ask students if they have ever heard or used any of these expressions, and if so, how and where. Next, tell the students that you are going to read the expressions again, and this time they are to listen for anything they have in common. Accept all answers, and then point out that all the expressions have something to do with the heart. Teach or review the definition of an *idiom*—an expression that means something other than what the words actually say. If you like, read the list a third time and let students speculate on what each idiom might really mean.

On the next page is a story that includes the *Ten to Teach* idioms. Note that the story is not intended to be an example of good writing; it would not be natural to use 10 idioms in such a short piece. The purpose of the story is simply to use all the expressions in context. The story is at approximately a 2.2 reading level. Use this information to read it aloud to students, have them read it, or both. This reproducible page includes the story and questions for students to answer related to the idioms used.

The final five pages of the unit introduce the basic *Ten to Teach* idioms individually, two to a page. These can be reproduced and used as is, or cut apart into separate cards. Use these after the story to reinforce the meanings of the idioms or to test students' understanding of them. Or, use them before the story as preparation for reading or for scaffolding as needed.

Optional: Use one of the ideas or activities in the introductory section of this book as an extension or follow-up to the unit.

Name _____ Date _____

Below is a story that includes ten idioms that use the word *heart*. Can you tell what they mean?

Grandma's Memory

I was watching some silly TV show when my mom came in. **With a heavy heart**, she told me the news. My grandma, her mom, had died. My **heart stood still**. I'd never seen my mom look so sad.

"Grandma had a **heart of gold**," I said, trying to make Mom feel better.

"Yes," Mom said **from the heart**. "Remember that time you had your **heart set on** baking her a birthday cake? You were only six. Although the cake didn't turn out, your **heart was in the right place**, and Grandma ate two pieces with a big smile. She **didn't have the heart** to tell you that it was pretty awful!"

Mom laughed a little, but I knew that she was **heartbroken** about Grandma. "We'll all miss Grandma very much," she said as her smile faded. "She was the **heart and soul** of the family." I gave Mom a hug.

"I know," I said with a little tear forming in the corner of my eye. "I'll always have a special **place in my heart** for her, too."

Read or listen to the story again. Then answer these questions about the idioms. To help you find them, the idioms are in **dark print** in the story.

1. Was the writer close to her grandma? How can you tell?

   _____

2. Why did Grandma eat the bad cake?

   _____

3. What "heart" idioms mean sad?

   _____

4. What did Mom mean when she said that Grandma was the **heart and soul** of the family?

   _____

5. Who is someone who holds a special place in your heart? Why is this person special to you?

   _____

   _____

Name _____ Date _____

Idiom ▶ **with a heavy heart**

Meaning ▶ sad; depressed

How It Is Used ▶ Susan and her family had a small ceremony when her hamster, Cuddles, died. *With a heavy heart*, she put him in a shoebox, which her dad buried in the backyard.

Which Is Right? ▶ Read the two selections. Choose the one in which *with a heavy heart* is used as an idiom. Circle the number of your choice.

❶ Samantha beamed when she gave her mom a Valentine's Day card she had made herself. The card was full of sequins, and in the middle was a *heavy heart* made of gem stones.

❷ Miles had been looking forward to going to the theme park for weeks. *With a heavy heart*, his mom explained, "I'm afraid we just can't go today. The thunderstorms will close down all the rides."

Idiom ▶ **heart stood still**

Meaning ▶ scared; shocked

How It Is Used ▶ Lisa couldn't wait to ride The Beast, the new roller coaster at the amusement park. Her *heart stood still* when the cars stopped at the top of the first hill, suspending the riders for a few moments before dropping them 120 feet at 65 miles per hour!

Which Is Right? ▶ Read the two selections. Choose the one in which *heart stood still* is used as an idiom. Circle the number of your choice.

❶ Sandy tried not to be grossed out by the frog she had to dissect. Much to her surprise, she was fascinated to see where its *heart stood still* along with all its other organs.

❷ Erin was worried when she heard that the principal was going to speak to her class. She thought they had done something wrong! Her *heart stood still* when Mrs. Eckert walked in, but she was relieved to hear the announcement that her class had won a pizza party for best attendance.

Name _____ Date _____

Idiom ▶ **heart of gold**

Meaning ▶ kind; nice; giving; thoughtful

How It Is Used ▶ Roger and Toby laugh to think that they were once afraid of their neighbor, Mr. Schmidt. He seemed mean when they first met him, but they have learned that he has a *heart of gold*.

Which Is Right? ▶ Read the two selections. Choose the one in which *heart of gold* is used as an idiom. Circle the number of your choice.

❶ During the holidays, Hannah and her mom worked as volunteers to collect food for families in need. They were happy to see how many people made donations. "There are so many people in our community who have a *heart of gold*," Hannah's mom said.

❷ Colleen enjoyed collecting charms for her bracelet. One day while shopping, she simply could not take her eyes off the charm with two silver hands holding a *heart of gold*.

Idiom ▶ **from the heart**

Meaning ▶ with meaning; sincere; thoughtful

How It Is Used ▶ Christy's dad really had no use for the handkerchief with painted hearts and flowers on it. Still, he kept it safely tucked away in his sock drawer for 20 years because he knew the gift from his niece was *from the heart*.

Which Is Right? ▶ Read the two selections. Choose the one in which *from the heart* is used as an idiom. Circle the number of your choice.

❶ Karen was nervous about the doctor taking X-rays to look at her heart. "This will let us see the blood flow to and *from the heart*. If something is wrong, we'll see it right away."

❷ Our music teacher was getting her chorus ready for a big concert. She played music with a lot of emotion to help the students learn how to sing with feeling. Once they heard the music, they were ready to sing *from the heart*.

Name _____ Date _____

Idiom ▶ **heart set on**

Meaning ▶ expect; determined to do something or get something

How It Is Used ▶ Blake stomped into his room and slammed his door. "He is just upset because he had his *heart set on* having his birthday party at the park," his mom explained to his dad. "Since it's raining, we'll have to do something else."

Which Is Right? ▶ Read the two selections. Choose the one in which *heart set on* is used as an idiom. Circle the number of your choice.

❶ Tina had her *heart set on* getting a new red bike for her birthday. She was somewhat disappointed when she walked outside and saw a shiny scooter with a big bow on it.

❷ The two girls watched in fascination as the doctor on the TV show carefully lifted the patient's new *heart set on* the tray, and put it into its new owner. Only time would tell if the operation was successful.

Idiom ▶ **heart in the right place**

Meaning ▶ kind and considerate, but may not show it; actions were kind, but the outcome didn't work out

How It Is Used ▶ The chocolate chip cookies Angelo made for the class looked great. When the class bit into them, they found them hard and slightly burnt. Most of the students didn't finish theirs, but his teacher, Mrs. Shaw, ate hers all up. They may not have tasted quite right, but she knew that Angelo had his *heart in the right place* when he made them.

Which Is Right? ▶ Read the two selections. Choose the one in which *heart in the right place* is used as an idiom. Circle the number of your choice.

❶ Mrs. Mayes found Geraldine's need to sharpen every pencil in her class pencil box a little aggravating, but she allowed her to do it since her *heart was in the right place*. All Geraldine really wanted was to know that if someone needed a pencil, it would be ready to use.

❷ The sci-fi movie I watched last night had a scene in which humans captured and studied aliens' bodies. Doctors could not find the lungs in the bodies, but their *hearts were in the right place*.

Name _____ Date _____

Idiom ▶	**didn't have the heart**
Meaning ▶	couldn't do something because a person didn't want to hurt someone's feelings
How It Is Used ▶	Jackie really wanted to know what her friend Kim thought of the story she wrote. Kim *didn't have the heart* to tell her it was really boring.
Which Is Right? ▶	Read the two selections. Choose the one in which *didn't have the heart* is used as an idiom. Circle the number of your choice.

❶ When Ben brought home a baby gerbil from his friend's house, his mom *didn't have the heart* to tell him he couldn't keep it. They spent the afternoon getting a gerbil cage, bedding, food, and care books so that Ben's new pet would be well cared for.

❷ Maggie and Liz were shopping for purses at the mall. Liz liked the one with the heart clasp, but Maggie preferred the one that *didn't have the heart* on it.

Idiom ▶	**heartbroken**
Meaning ▶	sad; grieving; disappointed
How It Is Used ▶	Joann and Terry had been best friends for three years. They were both heartbroken to learn that Terry's family was moving to another state, and that they would only be able to see each other once or twice a year.
Which Is Right? ▶	Read the two selections. Choose the one in which *heartbroken* is used as an idiom. Circle the number of your choice.

❶ Paul's mom wore a favorite silver heart on a chain around her neck every day. Last week she had her *heart broken* when my little brother pulled on it.

❷ Jeffery had spent months building a model of the Space Shuttle. He was *heartbroken* to find that his cat, Dunkin, had knocked it down and shattered the main frame.

Name _____ Date _____

Idiom ▶ **heart and soul**

Meaning ▶ with all your energy; with all your thought; completely; a person who is the center of a group

How It Is Used ▶ Marsha practiced every day for weeks for her piano recital. After her performance, many people told her parents that it sounded like she put her *heart and soul* into each piece.

Which Is Right? ▶ Read the two selections. Choose the one in which *heart and soul* is used as an idiom. Circle the number of your choice.

❶ At the church service, the minister spoke about generosity, and how it is good for the *heart and soul.*

❷ The students in the debate club at Gentry Middle School missed their teacher terribly after he retired. He was the *heart and soul* of the club. They weren't sure how they would perform without his support and guidance.

Idiom ▶ **place in one's heart**

Meaning ▶ have special meaning; be important to someone

How It Is Used ▶ With 10 foster children to look after, Mrs. Cain wasn't sure if she had a *place in her heart* for even one more child. But when she looked into Carl's lost and lonely eyes, she knew she would watch over him just as much as the others in her care.

Which Is Right? ▶ Read the two selections. Choose the one in which *place in one's heart* is used as an idiom. Circle the number of your choice.

❶ The horses at the stables all looked strong and healthy, and they were beautiful. But there was one, Lucky, that the owner had rescued from a burning barn as a colt. Lucky held a special *place in his heart.*

❷ Learning about the human body was interesting to Paul. "You have a *place in your heart* for valves, veins, and arteries," the textbook read. A detailed illustration labeled the parts of the heart.

Idioms With Feeling

This unit highlights idioms that show feeling. Below are two lists of idioms that focus on feelings. The first, *Ten to Teach*, presents the 10 expressions introduced and taught in this unit. The second, *More to Mention*, offers additional expressions in this theme that you may want to mention or use to create additional activities.

Ten to Teach

1. **wake up on the wrong side of the bed**
2. **rub someone the wrong way**
3. **on cloud nine**
4. **down in the dumps**
5. **in the hot seat**

X6. **run into a brick wall**
7. **out on a limb**
8. **flip one's lid**
9. **for the birds**
X10. **bent out of shape**

More to Mention

▶ walking on air
▶ blow a fuse
▶ bored stiff

▶ at the end of one's rope
▶ on the short end of the stick
X▶ have an ax to grind

▶ between a rock and a hard place
▶ up against the wall

Using This Unit

Begin by reading to students the basic *Ten to Teach* idioms. First, ask students if they have ever heard or used any of these expressions, and if so, how and where. Next, tell the students that you are going to read the expressions again, and this time they are to listen for anything they have in common. Accept all answers, and then point out that all the expressions show a feeling. Teach or review the definition of an *idiom*—an expression that means something other than what the words actually say. If you like, read the list a third time and let students speculate on which feeling each idiom expresses.

On the next page are three diary entries that include the *Ten to Teach* idioms. Note that it is not intended to be an example of good writing; it would not be natural to use 10 idioms in such a short piece. The purpose of the journal is simply to use all the expressions in context. The piece is at approximately a 1.9 reading level. Use this information to read it aloud to students, have them read it, or both. This reproducible page includes the story and questions for students to answer related to the idioms used.

The final five pages of the unit introduce the basic *Ten to Teach* idioms individually, two to a page. These can be reproduced and used as is, or cut apart into separate cards. Use these after the story to reinforce the meanings of the idioms or to test students' understanding of them. Or, use them before the story as preparation for reading or for scaffolding as needed.

Optional: Use one of the ideas or activities in the introductory section of this book as an extension or follow-up to the unit.

Name _____ Date _____

Below are three diary entries that include 10 idioms that show feeling. Can you tell which feelings they express?

January 29
Dear Diary,

   Maybe I just **woke up on the wrong side of the bed**. I was in a bad mood all day. Everything just seemed to **rub me the wrong way**. To top it off, report cards came out and my sister got straight As. She was walking around **on cloud nine** and acting pretty annoying. Nobody noticed that I was **down in the dumps**.

February 2
Dear Diary,

   It snowed last night. This morning Mom said, "Do you know what today is?"

   I instantly thought, "Uh-oh. I'm forgetting something important—like her birthday or something." No, that's later this month. To buy more time, I said, "February second?"

   "Yes, but that's not what I meant," she replied.

   I was **in the hot seat** now. I had to think fast, but I **ran into a brick wall**. Then I got an idea! I went **out on a limb** and said, "A snow day? No school?"

   "Sorry, but that's not it," she answered. "It's Groundhog Day, and he didn't see his shadow, so spring will be here soon!"

   I looked out the window. The snow was really coming down. Sometimes I wonder if that woman has **flipped her lid**.

February 14
Dear Diary,

   I think Valentine's Day is **for the birds**. This girl in my class gave me one of those silly cards that said, "You're Cool! Be Mine?" Then she got all **bent out of shape** when I didn't look thrilled.

Read or listen to the entries again. Then answer these questions about the idioms. To help you find them, the idioms are in **dark print** in the text.

1. Was January 29 a good day or a bad day? _____

2. Was the author of the diary thrilled that his sister got good grades or annoyed with her?

   _____

3. Was the writer able to figure out what was so special about February 2?

   _____

4. The author of the diary thinks Valentine's Day is **for the birds**. What's something you think is **for the birds**? _____

Name _____ Date _____

Idiom ▶ **wake up on the wrong side of the bed**

Meaning ▶ to feel grumpy or annoyed

How It Is Used ▶ In class, Madelyn's teacher asked if she would like to take down the chairs around the room, a chore she usually enjoyed in the morning. "Not today," Madelyn mumbled as she slumped in her seat. Since Madelyn didn't seem like her usual, perky self, her teacher figured she must have *woken up on the wrong side of the bed*.

Which Is Right? ▶ Read the two selections. Choose the one in which *wake up on the wrong side of the bed* is used as an idiom. Circle the number of your choice.

❶ Grandma always placed her slippers at her bedside at night so they would be there when she woke up in the morning. One morning she came to breakfast without them. "Where are your slippers, Grandma?" I asked. She explained that they weren't handy since she had *woken up on the wrong side of the bed*.

❷ The director of the play was excited about opening night. Much to his surprise, the lead actor seemed to be in a bad mood during rehearsals. One of the stage helpers mentioned that he must have *woken up on the wrong side of the bed*.

Idiom ▶ **rub someone the wrong way**

Meaning ▶ bother; annoy; dislike

How It Is Used ▶ The neighbor's dog sometimes runs around the neighborhood without a leash. My mom usually makes me come inside because she says that something about the dog *rubs her the wrong way*.

Which Is Right? ▶ Read the two selections. Choose the one in which *rub someone the wrong way* is used as an idiom. Circle the number of your choice.

❶ My teacher keeps small rodents and fish as class pets. When we asked if we could also keep a lizard or snake, she shivered a polite no, explaining that those kinds of creatures *rub her the wrong way*.

❷ I offered to help my brother wax his new car, but he said he would do it himself. He said that last time I *rubbed it the wrong way*.

Name _____ Date _____

Idiom	▶	**on cloud nine**
Meaning	▶	elated; excited; pleased; happy
How It Is Used	▶	Bianca knew that getting "first chair" in the school band was going to be tough because everyone was so good at playing the flute. She was *on cloud nine* when her band director announced that she would hold that seat for the concert!
Which Is Right?	▶	Read the two selections. Choose the one in which *on cloud nine* is used as an idiom. Circle the number of your choice.

❶ The kindergartners were learning their numbers. Their teacher had little numbered cutouts on the floor for practice. When lining up to go to lunch, she told Mona, "Go stand *on cloud nine*."

❷ Fred enjoyed nothing more than studying rocks and gems. When his class went on a trip to the science museum, he was *on cloud nine* when they reached the gems and minerals room.

Idiom	▶	**down in the dumps**
Meaning	▶	depressed; sad
How It Is Used	▶	My friend Ben was *down in the dumps* after failing our math test.
Which Is Right?	▶	Read the two selections. Choose the one in which *down in the dumps* is used as an idiom. Circle the number of your choice.

❶ I figured that my sister would be happy when her team won the championships. Instead, she was *down in the dumps* because she had to sit on the bench for most of the game.

❷ My uncle works as a sanitation worker, collecting garbage. Once, a woman asked him to go *down in the dumps* to find a diamond ring she accidentally threw away!

Idioms With Feeling (cont.)

Name _____ Date _____

Idiom ▶ **in the hot seat**

Meaning ▶ in a situation where one has to perform his or her best, or do well

How It Is Used ▶ The math competition was a close match. Our team was tied with the other team. This last question would decide the contest. The problem was given to my friend, Carl. He was really *in the hot seat*!

Which Is Right? ▶ Read the two selections. Choose the one in which *in the hot seat* is used as an idiom. Circle the number of your choice.

❶ When my older sister came in late for the third night in a row, Dad was waiting for her. She was really *in the hot seat*! If she didn't have a good excuse, she could look forward to being grounded for a long time.

❷ The seat warmers in my mom's new car are great. There's nothing as nice as getting into the car on a freezing winter morning and sitting *in the hot seat*.

Idiom ▶ **run into a brick wall**

Meaning ▶ when something happens to stop a person from doing something or getting somewhere important

How It Is Used ▶ Little sisters can be so rude! Every time I want to tell Grandpa an important story, she interrupts me. My stories always seem to *run into a brick wall*.

Which Is Right? ▶ Read the two selections. Choose the one in which *run into a brick wall* is used as an idiom. Circle the number of your choice.

❶ Jason's new skateboard was fast! He told his mom he would be down the street showing off to his friends. She warned him to be careful not to hit a car or *run into a brick wall*.

❷ As the museum workers attempted to piece together a new dinosaur fossil, they discovered they were missing a few essential bones. Unless the pieces were found, the project would *run into a brick wall*.

Name _____ Date _____

Idiom ▶ **go out on a limb**

Meaning ▶ when a person guesses, knowing that he or she will probably be wrong; to put oneself in a risky position in order to help another person

How It Is Used ▶ Math used to be easy, but this new kind of problem confused a lot of students. When the teacher called for the answers to the homework, only a few students were willing to *go out on a limb* and give their solutions.

Which Is Right? ▶ Read the two selections. Choose the one in which *go out on a limb* is used as an idiom. Circle the number of your choice.

❶ Everyone watched in delight as the new monkeys at the zoo entertained their guests by going *out on a limb* and swinging from tree to tree.

❷ "How many stars are in the sky?" Dana asked Janet. Not knowing the first thing about the universe, Janet *went out on a limb* and guessed, "A million trillion."

Idiom ▶ **flip one's lid**

Meaning ▶ get angry or upset; go mad or crazy

How It Is Used ▶ After a bad pitch at the baseball game hit the batter, a fight broke out among all of the players. "The guys have *flipped their lids*!" my dad yelled.

Which Is Right? ▶ Read the two selections. Choose the one in which *flip one's lid* is used as an idiom. Circle the number of your choice.

❶ Cooking class was always fun. One student tried to *flip the lid* to his pot, but the lid landed wrong. Once he flipped it, he was ready to cook.

❷ My brother's friend was kind of angry after his new headphones were stolen from his locker. But when someone stole his cell phone, he really *flipped his lid.*

Idioms With Feeling *(cont.)*

Name _____ Date _____

Idiom ▶ **for the birds**

Meaning ▶ totally uninteresting and meaningless

How It Is Used ▶ Roger's birthday party was supposed to include a great magician. When a clown showed up who did silly little kid games and tricks, Roger's friends got up, exclaiming, "This act is *for the birds*."

Which Is Right? ▶ Read the two selections. Choose the one in which *for the birds* is used as an idiom. Circle the number of your choice.

❶ The Jones family was looking forward to horseback riding while on vacation. When they got to the stables, the wrangler wanted to put Chris on a pony. "A pony!" the 10-year-old exclaimed. "That's *for the birds*."

❷ The garden was perfect. It had just the right blooming plants for the bees and butterflies and special feeding areas *for the birds*.

Idiom ▶ **bent out of shape**

Meaning ▶ upset; offended; to have one's feelings hurt

How It Is Used ▶ "The last ice cream cone was mine!" Harold shouted to his older brother, Steve. Just then, the boys' mom came in. "Don't get *bent out of shape*," she reassured Harold. "There's a new box in the back of the freezer."

Which Is Right? ▶ Read the two selections. Choose the one in which *bent out of shape* is used as an idiom. Circle the number of your choice.

❶ David bought his mom a pair of dangling earrings for her birthday. But when he got them home, he could see that one of the earring wires was *bent out of shape*.

❷ Tommy expected to be invited to Jacob's birthday party. When the invitations were handed out and he didn't receive one, he was *bent out of shape*.

   © Shell Education

This unit highlights idioms that are related to water and weather. Below are two lists of idioms that focus on water and weather. The first, *Ten to Teach*, presents the 10 expressions introduced and taught in this unit. The second, *More to Mention*, offers additional expressions in this theme that you may want to mention or use to create additional activities.

Ten to Teach

1. under the weather
2. raining cats and dogs
3. soaked to the bone
4. usual sunny self
5. like water off a duck's back

6. in a fog
7. misty-eyed
8. a flood of tears
9. burning up (with fever)
10. in hot water

More to Mention

▶ sky-high temperature*
▶ a wet blanket*
▶ wash away the tears*
▶ a snow job

▶ an icy stare
▶ all steamed up
▶ turn on the waterworks
▶ on the sunny side of the street

▶ rain on someone's parade
▶ as fresh as springtime

These idioms are also included in the story but are not highlighted individually in the unit.

Using This Unit

Begin by reading to students the basic *Ten to Teach* idioms. First, ask students if they have ever heard or used any of these expressions, and if so, how and where. Next, read the expressions again, and this time the students are to listen for anything they have in common. Be sure they point out that all the expressions have to do with water or the weather. Teach or review the definition of an *idiom*—an expression that means something other than what the words actually say. Read the list a third time and let students speculate on what each idiom might really mean.

On the next page is a story that includes the *Ten to Teach* idioms (along with three *More to Mention* idioms). Note that it is not intended to be an example of good writing; it would not be natural to use 13 idioms in such a short piece. The purpose of the story is simply to use all the expressions in context. The story is at approximately a 4.9 reading level. Use this information to read it aloud to students, have them read it, or both. This reproducible page includes the story and questions for students to answer related to the idioms used.

The final five pages of the unit introduce the basic *Ten to Teach* idioms individually, two to a page. These can be reproduced and used as is, or cut apart into separate cards. Use these after the story to reinforce the meanings of the idioms or to test students' understanding of them. Or, use them before the story as preparation for reading or for scaffolding as needed.

Optional: Use one of the ideas or activities in the introductory section of this book as an extension or follow-up to the unit.

Name _____ Date _____

Below is a story that includes 13 idioms related to water and weather. Can you tell what they mean?

Too Sick to Test

Jenny had a big social studies test coming up on Friday. Thursday evening she started feeling **under the weather**. Earlier in the day, it had **rained cats and dogs** and she got **soaked to the bone** walking home from school. Even though she wasn't feeling like her **usual sunny self**, she had to study. She tried to let how she was feeling roll off her **like water off a duck's back** and kept studying. As she struggled to learn the social studies words, she felt as if her brain were **in a fog**. She dutifully pressed on, but began to feel worse and worse. **Misty-eyed**, she wondered how she was going to learn all the terms in time for the test the next day. She wiped away one tear and then another, but then came a **flood of tears**.

Her mom heard Jenny's sobs and came in to her room. As soon as she saw Jenny, she went to get the thermometer. Sure enough, her **temperature was sky-high** and she was **burning up** with fever.

Mom immediately told Jenny to get into bed. Jenny protested, saying that she would be **in hot water** if she didn't keep studying.

"I hate to be a **wet blanket**," said her mom, "But there will be no test tomorrow—not for you! You are staying home until this fever breaks. Now **wash away those tears** and get some rest, young lady."

With that, Mom tucked Jenny in and gave her a kiss on the forehead. Jenny smiled, not just because Mom's cool lips on her warm skin felt good, but more because she knew her Mom loved her and would take care of her. And that was more important than any test.

Read or listen to the story again. Then answer these questions about the idioms. To help you find them, the idioms are in **dark print** in the story.

1. What caused Jenny to get sick? _____

2. What symptom of illness did Jenny have? _____

3. How did Jenny react as she tried to study? _____

4. What did Jenny think would happen if she didn't study?

   _____

5. Jenny tried not to let how she felt stop her from studying. Describe a time when you tried to let something roll off you **like water off a duck's back**.

   _____

Name _____ Date _____

Idiom ▶ **under the weather**

Meaning ▶ sick; ill; not feeling well

How It Is Used ▶ Fluffy was *under the weather*. She usually wagged her tail and teased her owners to play. Today she mostly slept and whined. Fluffy's owner finally called the veterinarian to schedule an appointment.

Which Is Right? ▶ Read the two selections. Choose the one in which *under the weather* is used as an idiom. Circle the number of your choice.

❶ Our family was supposed to go on a picnic on Sunday. But our mom woke up feeling *under the weather*, so we postponed our picnic for another day.

❷ Our teacher kept many kinds of maps in the classroom. *Under the weather* map, she kept world maps, a map of the solar system, and even a map of our school!

Idiom ▶ **raining cats and dogs**

Meaning ▶ pour down rain; rain hard

How It Is Used ▶ "Since it is *raining cats and dogs*, let's go to the movies today," Marsha's mom suggested. Marsha grabbed the phone and called a friend to join them.

Which Is Right? ▶ Read the two selections. Choose the one in which *raining cats and dogs* is used as an idiom. Circle the number of your choice.

❶ The cartoon show was a favorite of the two girls. They laughed out loud when the airplane *rained cats and dogs* wearing parachutes down upon the pet shop. This was how the shop received its shipments of new animals!

❷ Ryan asked his mom if he could go outside to play, but his mom wouldn't let him. "Haven't you looked outside?" she asked. "It's *raining cats and dogs*!"

Name _____ Date _____

Idiom ▶ **soaked to the bone**

Meaning ▶ very wet; so wet as to seem never to dry

How It Is Used ▶ John was kind to mow the Frost's yard while they were away on vacation. But before even half the yard was done, John found himself surprised by the Frost's sprinkler system, and he got *soaked to the bone*.

Which Is Right? ▶ Read the two selections. Choose the one in which *soaked to the bone* is used as an idiom. Circle the number of your choice.

❶ While walking downtown, a fire hydrant burst, showering the entire corner of First and Fifth Streets. We wound up *soaked to the bone* by the gushing water.

❷ Step two of the recipe read: "Place your chicken in a bowl with buttermilk, and *soak to the bone* of the chicken, at least three hours, or overnight."

Idiom ▶ **usual sunny self**

Meaning ▶ a person who is happy or smiles a lot; a person who makes other people happy

How It Is Used ▶ Viewers tuned in every day to watch their local newscaster deliver the news. Not only did they learn what was happening in their community, but the newscaster was always her *usual sunny self*. Those who watched her left their homes in a good mood, ready for the day.

Which Is Right? ▶ Read the two selections. Choose the one in which *usual sunny self* is used as an idiom. Circle the number of your choice.

❶ Radio broadcast: "It's another hot day out there, with the sun its *usual sunny self*, beaming down on our town. Be sure to wear plenty of sunscreen today, folks, and keep the water coming."

❷ Michelle was nervous before she gave her speech to the students at Rockville Elementary School. But as she shared her ideas about school improvements, she was her *usual sunny self*. Her positive outlook gave her a quiet confidence that her classmates liked.

Name _____ Date _____

Idiom ▶ **like water off a duck's back**

Meaning ▶ when something has no effect on a person; when something does not bother someone

How It Is Used ▶ The Bush family's dog, Cobb, was great with little children. Baby Emma would tug and pull on his fur, tail, and ears, but Cobb never bit, nipped, or even growled. The family liked that Cobb could let the annoyance roll off him *like water off a duck's back*.

Which Is Right? ▶ Read the two selections. Choose the one in which *like water off a duck's back* is used as an idiom. Circle the number of your choice.

❶ A marine biologist visited our classroom to show the effects of oil spills on birds that live in water. "As you can see, the oil sticks to the feathers, and doesn't allow the *water to roll off the duck's back*."

❷ Good comedians never let the audience bother them. They have a way of letting comments and jeers roll off them *like water off a duck's back*. Sometimes they might even be quick-witted enough to use the jeers as part of the comedy routine.

Idiom ▶ **in a fog**

Meaning ▶ unknowing; unaware; confused; sad or depressed

How It Is Used ▶ Raul had always wanted to visit the big city. He had spent all 12 years of his life in a small town where everyone knew one another. When he first stepped off the bus in Dallas, there were so many lights, noises, and people, it seemed as if his head were *in a fog*.

Which Is Right? ▶ Read the two selections. Choose the one in which *in a fog* is used as an idiom. Circle the number of your choice.

❶ Beth and her dog had been together since Beth was born. After 15 years, Boots had died. Beth walked around *in a fog* for over a week, feeling sad and empty without her best friend.

❷ The young children on the bus had learned a great trick. They breathed on the bus window, then wrote their letters *in a fog* that condensed on the window.

Name _____   Date _____

Idiom ▶ **misty-eyed**

Meaning ▶ having tears in a person's eyes, but not shedding tears; having strong emotions (from an event that may make a person cry)

How It Is Used ▶ Itty Bitty Daycare had practiced for many weeks for their preschool graduation ceremony. All the moms and dads looked on, many of them *misty-eyed*, knowing their young children would soon be in kindergarten.

Which Is Right? ▶ Read the two selections. Choose the one in which *misty-eyed* is used as an idiom. Circle the number of your choice.

❶ The final scene in the movie was quite sad. Most, if not all, of the moviegoers left the theater *misty-eyed*.

❷ At the carnival, a clown came up and surprised us by spraying us with a water gun, leaving me *misty-eyed* and in need of a towel.

Idiom ▶ **a flood of tears**

Meaning ▶ crying endlessly; crying for a long time

How It Is Used ▶ The teenager was arrested for stealing a car. After hours of questioning, *in a flood of tears*, he confessed to the crime.

Which Is Right? ▶ Read the two selections. Choose the one in which a *flood of tears* is used as an idiom. Circle the number of your choice.

❶ The Pearson's new house was supposed to be done at the end of the month. Mrs. Pearson couldn't wait to see it. When she walked in and saw that the house was still months away from completion, she ran out in *a flood of tears*.

❷ "What are you doing with the salt and the water?" Mom asked. "We are making salt water for our Indian play set," I explained. "We want a *flood of tears* to come down over the village during a ceremonial dance."

Name _____ Date _____

Idiom ▶ **burning up (with fever)**

Meaning ▶ having a high fever; very hot from a high fever

How It Is Used ▶ The school nurse called with concern in her voice. "Your daughter, Emily, is in our clinic," she explained. "She is *burning up* with a 103.8° fever." Emily's mom promised to be right there. Before she left the house, she called Emily's doctor for an appointment.

Which Is Right? ▶ Read the two selections. Choose the one in which *burning up* is used as an idiom. Circle the number of your choice.

❶ We watched from down the road as the abandoned house was *burning up*. The fire department was already there, trying to control the flames.

❷ My baby sister was crying most of the night. We just thought she was being fussy. But when Mom checked on her, she found that she was *burning up* with fever.

Idiom ▶ **in hot water**

Meaning ▶ in trouble; in a situation that may bring punishment

How It Is Used ▶ Brian was so busy with sports that his grades were falling. If he didn't start working harder in school, he was going to be *in hot water* with his parents.

Which Is Right? ▶ Read the two selections. Choose the one in which *in hot water* is used as an idiom. Circle the number of your choice.

❶ When he got home from a hard day at work, the gardener liked to shower *in hot water* to remove all the dirt and grime.

❷ The grocery store cashier stole a few dollars from her register each night before closing, but she didn't think anyone would notice. One night, when she went into the office to turn in her drawer, she was surprised to see a police officer. She realized then that she was *in hot water* with the law.

Idioms About Objects

This unit highlights idioms about objects. Below are two lists of idioms that focus on objects. The first, *Ten to Teach*, presents the 10 expressions introduced and taught in this unit. The second, *More to Mention*, offers additional expressions in this theme that you may want to mention or use to create additional activities.

Ten to Teach

1. piece of cake
2. hit the hay
3. in the driver's seat
4. blow a fuse
5. the short end of the stick

6. leave in the dust
7. hands down
8. second fiddle
9. hats off
10. in the bag

More to Mention

▶ couch potato*
▶ ham it up*
▶ humble pie*

▶ flew the coop
▶ bark up the wrong tree
▶ on the fence

▶ walk on eggs
▶ in the same boat
▶ be a fly on the wall

These idioms are also included in the story but are not highlighted individually in the unit.

Using This Unit

Begin by reading to students the basic *Ten to Teach* idioms. First, ask students if they have ever heard or used any of these expressions, and if so, how and where. Next, tell the students that you are going to read the expressions again, and this time they are to listen for anything they have in common. Accept all answers, and then point out that all the expressions have to do with objects (things). Teach or review the definition of an *idiom*—an expression that means something other than what the words actually say. If you like, read the list a third time and let students speculate on what each idiom might really mean.

On the next page is a letter that includes the *Ten to Teach* idioms (along with three *More to Mention* idioms). Note that it is not intended to be an example of good writing; it would not be natural to use 13 idioms in such a short piece. The purpose of the text is simply to use all the expressions in context. The letter is at approximately a 3.3 reading level. Use this information to read it aloud to students, have them read it, or both. This reproducible page includes the story and questions for students to answer related to the idioms used.

The final five pages of the unit introduce the basic *Ten to Teach* idioms individually, two to a page. These can be reproduced and used as is, or cut apart into separate cards. Use these after the story to reinforce the meanings of the idioms or test students' understanding of them. Or, use them before the story as preparation for reading or for scaffolding as needed.

Optional: Use one of the ideas or activities in the introductory section of this book as an extension or follow-up to the unit.

Name _____ Date _____

Below is a letter that includes 13 idioms about objects. Can you tell what they mean?

Turn of Events

Dear Jason,

We had field day at school last week. You know I am no **couch potato**. I love to compete, especially in sports. Winning something at field day would be a **piece of cake!**

The night before, I **hit the hay** early. I wanted to be **in the driver's seat** when the competition began.

The first event was the three-legged sack race. When I got Becky as my partner, I was a little nervous. We started hopping down the field and people were tripping and falling all over the place. To my surprise, Becky had great balance and we didn't trip at all. Becky and I left everyone else behind and crossed the finish line first! We really **hammed it up** when the rest came crawling in.

Next was the relay race. There had to be a boy and a girl on each team. Of all people, Margie was paired with me. I just about **blew a fuse**. She is so small and I have never seen her walk fast, let alone run. I convinced her to go first, thinking that I would make up any time she lost for us. Boy, did I give her **the short end of the stick**! She took off running and **left the others in the dust**. When she handed the flag off to me, there was no one even close to us. We beat everyone **hands down**.

I used to think girls were **second fiddle** in sports competitions. I hate to admit it, but this field day, I ate some **humble pie**! The girls were just as competitive as the boys! So I say, "**Hats off** to Becky and Margie!" Without them as my partners, I may not have had these wins **in the bag**.

Your friend,

Brandon

Read or listen to the story again. Then answer these questions about the idioms. To help you find them, the idioms are in **dark print** in the story.

1. How did Brandon prepare for field day? _____

2. How did Brandon react when he was paired with Margie for the relay race?

   _____

3. Why did Brandon say he gave Margie the **short end of the stick**?

   _____

4. Did Brandon expect the girls to do well in the field day competitions?

   _____

5. How do you think Brandon treated Becky and Margie before field day? How might his attitude toward the girls be different now? _____

Name _____ Date _____

Idiom ▶ **piece of cake**

Meaning ▶ easy to do; something that requires no effort

How It Is Used ▶ Jacob was known for his steady hand and keen eye. He and his friends played a game where they had to pull out an object from the game board without setting off the alarm. When Jacob learned the rules, he smiled and thought, "This will be a *piece of cake*."

Which Is Right? ▶ Read the two selections. Choose the one in which *piece of cake* is used as an idiom. Circle the number of your choice.

❶ Once Rhonda had mastered all the multiplication facts, her teacher told the class they had a test the next day. "This should be a *piece of cake*," Rhonda thought.

❷ The party at the roller rink was going well. After skating, everyone had some pizza and then had a *piece of cake*.

Idiom ▶ **hit the hay**

Meaning ▶ go to bed; go to sleep

How It Is Used ▶ My friends and I decided our regular sleepover would be better if we camped in the backyard. It was almost midnight when my mom popped her head inside the tent. "It's time to *hit the hay*, boys," she said.

Which Is Right? ▶ Read the two selections. Choose the one in which *hit the hay* is used as an idiom. Circle the number of your choice.

❶ I enjoyed spending time on my cousin's farm, but it was hard work. First we woke up really early, at sunrise. Then we took care of the animals. Next we *hit the hay*, cleaning and refilling the horse stalls with fresh hay. Finally, it was time for lunch.

❷ Our day on the water was a lot of fun, but all that time in the sun was tiring. Just a couple of hours after dinner, my dad mumbled, "I'm ready to *hit the hay*."

Name _____ Date _____

Idiom ▶ **in the driver's seat**

Meaning ▶ in control of something; having an advantage

How It Is Used ▶ "Halibut's does a really good business," my friend noted. "They carry supplies for unusual reptiles and amphibians. They also carry saltwater fish and exotic birds. Being the only pet shop in town to have these odd animals really puts them *in the driver's seat.*"

Which Is Right? ▶ Read the two selections. Choose the one in which *in the driver's seat* is used as an idiom. Circle the number of your choice.

❶ My dad was looking all over for his car keys. I offered to help and started looking all over the house. It wasn't until I went out to the car that I looked through the window and saw them *in the driver's seat.*

❷ Eddie has a batting cage in his backyard. When our team wants to practice, Eddie gets to decide the time. Owning the batting cage really puts him *in the driver's seat.*

Idiom ▶ **blow a fuse**

Meaning ▶ become suddenly angry; get mad

How It Is Used ▶ Mom had let me use her credit card to buy new school clothes. She was always careful with her money. She gave me a limit and told me to not go over it. She is going to *blow a fuse* when she finds out how much I spent.

Which Is Right? ▶ Read the two selections. Choose the one in which *blow a fuse* is used as an idiom. Circle the number of your choice.

❶ Richard *blew a fuse* when he found out his little sister had been in his room. "This sign clearly says DO NOT ENTER!" he shouted at her. "Richard, leave her alone," Mom said. "You know your baby sister can't read."

❷ My friends and I like to fix up our hair when we sleep over. Last time, we had so many hair dryers and curling irons plugged in, Dad was worried we'd *blow a fuse.*

Name _____ Date _____

Idiom ▶ **the short end of the stick**

Meaning ▶ to suffer the bad effects of a situation; to not give credit to someone

How It Is Used ▶ Aunt Jill was never very good at cutting a cake into even pieces. The last person served got *the short end of the stick*. That piece was always the smallest and had the least amount of frosting.

Which Is Right? ▶ Read the two selections. Choose the one in which *the short end of the stick* is used as an idiom. Circle the number of your choice.

❶ Robin and Kathy like to go sledding. Since Kathy was so much smaller than Robin, Robin got *the short end of the stick*. She was the one who had to drag the sled up the hill for the two girls. The effort was worth it, though. They always had a great time together.

❷ Rather than decide by "Rock, Paper, Scissors," our soccer team liked to draw sticks. The person who got the *short end of the stick* had to be the referee.

Idiom ▶ **leave in the dust**

Meaning ▶ move quickly ahead of someone or something; to be much better than someone or something else

How It Is Used ▶ Brooke was excited about her present. "Look at the graphics and action. This new Allegro 3000 *leaves* my last video game *in the dust*!" she exclaimed.

Which Is Right? ▶ Read the two selections. Choose the one in which *leave in the dust* is used as an idiom. Circle the number of your choice.

❶ Victor couldn't wait to get to the go-cart track. He intended to *leave everyone in the dust*. Not even his dad would be able to catch up to him!

❷ "Oh, Bobby, that nickel is so dirty," his mom scolded. "Please don't pick it up. Just *leave it in the dust*. I'll give you a shiny new one when we get home," she offered.

#50159—Idioms and Other English Expressions © Shell Education

Name _____ Date _____

Idiom ▶ **hands down**

Meaning ▶ without difficulty; easily; certainly (usually to win something)

How It Is Used ▶ The students were about to elect their new class president. Hilary had the best posters, made the best speech, and everyone liked her. We were all sure she would win *hands down*.

Which Is Right? ▶ Read the two selections. Choose the one in which *hands down* is used as an idiom. Circle the number of your choice.

❶ As the teacher read from the social studies textbook, she asked students to keep their *hands down* until after she was done. "I'll take questions after I'm finished reading," she said.

❷ "Why did you challenge Vera to a tennis match?" Gail asked herself. "She has been taking lessons for two years and has won three trophies. She is going to beat you *hands down*."

Idiom ▶ **second fiddle**

Meaning ▶ someone who is not as good or who is not considered as important as someone else

How It Is Used ▶ David was tired of playing *second fiddle* to Charles, who always seemed to get better days off and more pay. Finally, David had the courage to quit his job and start his own business.

Which Is Right? ▶ Read the two selections. Choose the one in which *second fiddle* is used as an idiom. Circle the number of your choice.

❶ The square dance was getting people of all ages to get up and move. When the group became too large, someone picked up a *second fiddle* so another square could form in another area of the barn.

❷ The co-stars of the movie shared top billing, but tensions started running high when one star felt he was playing *second fiddle* to his younger co-star.

Idioms About Objects (cont.)

Name _____ Date _____

Idiom ▶ **hats off**

Meaning ▶ what a person says to give credit to someone, or show admiration or approval

How It Is Used ▶ Bryce thanked his mom for the great surprise birthday party. "*Hats off* to your friend Kevin," his mom explained. "It was all his idea. He planned it and invited all your friends."

Which Is Right? ▶ Read the two selections. Choose the one in which *hats off* is used as an idiom. Circle the number of your choice.

❶ The Gordon family was looking forward to enjoying a movie together. They had to get up and change their seats when a group of teenagers sat down in front of them. Even when asked to do so, they refused to stop talking or even take their *hats off*. The Gordon's two children couldn't see the screen.

❷ "This class picnic was a great idea," Mandell told his teacher. "*Hats off* to the class for thinking of it," his teacher responded. "This will definitely be something I do with my class each year."

Idiom ▶ **in the bag**

Meaning ▶ a sure thing; something that will certainly happen

How It Is Used ▶ "We're at the bottom of the sixth inning," the sports announcer said. "The Tornados have just scored their tenth run of the game. The Daisies have just one run on the board. The game's not over, folks, but it seems the Tornados have this one *in the bag*."

Which Is Right? ▶ Read the two selections. Choose the one in which *in the bag* is used as an idiom. Circle the number of your choice.

❶ Amy and Emily cheered for their school at the regional geography competition. "Our team is by far the best," Emily said confidently. "We have this win *in the bag*."

❷ "Mom! I can't find my blue hair band with the white dots," Jenny called. "I saw it yesterday," Jenny's mom said. "Look *in the bag* by the front door."

This unit highlights idioms that are similes. Below are two lists of similes. The first, *Ten to Teach*, presents the 10 similes introduced and taught in this unit. The second, *More to Mention*, offers additional similes that you may want to mention or use to create additional activities.

Ten to Teach

1. **as different as night and day**
2. **like a bump on a log**
3. **as hungry as a bear**
4. **eats like a horse**
5. **as strong as an ox**

6. **as sweet as honey**
7. **eat like a bird**
8. **feel/look like a million bucks**
9. **like the icing on the cake**
10. **as stubborn as a mule**

More to Mention

▶ like a hog*
▶ as snug as a bug in a rug
▶ as sick as a dog
▶ as gentle as a lamb

▶ like a fish out of water
▶ as cute as a button
▶ as solid as a rock
▶ (run) like the wind

▶ as wise as an owl
▶ as cool as a cucumber

This simile is also included in the poem but is not highlighted individually in the unit.

Using This Unit

Begin by reading to students the basic *Ten to Teach* similes. First, ask students if they have ever heard or used any of these expressions, and if so, how and where. Next, tell the students that you are going to read the expressions again, and this time they are to listen for anything they have in common. Accept all answers, and then point out that all the expressions compare one thing to another. Teach or review the definition of a *simile*—a comparison using *like* or *as*. If you like, read the list a third time and let students identify the comparison in each simile.

On the next page is a poem that includes the *Ten to Teach* similes (along with one *More to Mention* simile). Note that the poem is not intended to be an example of good writing; it would not be natural to use 11 similes in such a short piece. The purpose of the poem is simply to use all the expressions in context. The poem is at approximately a 1.0 reading level. This reproducible page includes the poem and questions for students to answer related to the similes used.

The final five pages of the unit introduce the basic *Ten to Teach* similes individually, two to a page. These can be reproduced and used as is, or cut apart into separate cards. Use these after the poem to reinforce the meanings of the similes or to test students' understanding of them. Or, use them before the story as preparation for reading or for scaffolding as needed.

Note: Instead of identifying which example uses the phrase as an idiom, as in previous units in this book, students are asked questions that lead them to decide whether or not a phrase in a selection is used as a simile.

Optional: Use one of the ideas or activities in the introductory section of this book as an extension or follow up to the unit.

Name _____ Date _____

Below is a poem containing 11 similes. Can you tell what they are comparing?

Breakfast Blues

Every morning it's the same,
Brothers **as different as night and day**.
Tim gobbles his breakfast down **like a hog**
While Tom just sits **like a bump on a log**.

"You have to eat!" says Tommy's mother.
"Why can't you be more like your brother?
You must be **as hungry as a bear**
Yet you just sit there and stare.

Your brother Tim **eats like a horse**;
Cleans his plate of every course.
Although he hardly ever talks,
He is **as strong as an ox**!

You are **as sweet as honey** in a word,
But honey, *you* **eat like a bird**!
Good food will help you grow and feel
Like a million bucks—that's the deal.

More energy to work and play,
Not feel so sleepy through the day.
Smarter too, not just awake
Could be **like the icing on the cake**!

Tommy Turner—as a rule
You're **as stubborn as a mule**!
Now before you go out the door
Pick up that spoon and eat some more!"

Read or listen to the poem again. Then answer these questions about the similes. To help you find them, the similes are in **dark print** in the story.

1. To which animals is Tim compared? To which animals is Tom compared?

   _____

2. Which animal comparison do you think is the best fit for each brother?

   _____

3. What does the twins' mother compare to **icing on the cake**?

   _____

4. If you were Tommy, what would persuade you to eat?

   _____

Name _____   Date _____

Simile ▶ as different as night and day

Meaning ▶ being opposites; not alike

How It Is Used ▶ Our dog had two puppies that looked identical. Both were black with a white patch. But they were *as different as night and day*. One was outgoing and loved to be held by people and the other was very shy and scared around people.

Recognizing Similes ▶ **Remember: A simile is a comparison using *like* or *as*.**
Read the selection. Answer the questions below.

Mona thought all campgrounds were pretty much the same. She discovered last summer that they can be *as different as night and day*. At her family's first stop, they camped in a campground that had lush trees, a refreshing lake, and clean bathrooms. The next night they found themselves camping in the hot sun with no relief from the heat, and there was nothing more than a water pump and an outhouse to use to clean up.

❶ Is something being compared to something else?   ○ yes   ○ no

❷ Is the word *like* or *as* used to compare?   ○ yes   ○ no

❸ Are the words *different as night and day* part of a simile in this selection?   ○ yes ○ no

---

Simile ▶ like a bump on a log

Meaning ▶ unmoving; not active; sits around a lot or doesn't get involved in things

How It Is Used ▶ My brother hasn't wanted to do anything or go anywhere this summer. He just sits around *like a bump on a log* watching TV or playing video games.

Recognizing Similes ▶ **Remember: A simile is a comparison using *like* or *as*.**
Read the selection. Answer the questions below.

Our soccer coach can really get us moving! First we do warm-ups to loosen our muscles and get our blood pumping. Then we move onto drills to practice dribbling, passing, and shooting. For a full 90 minutes, we are moving, moving, moving. Soccer is definitely not a game for people who prefer to act *like a bump on a log*.

❶ Is something being compared to something else?   ○ yes   ○ no

❷ Is the word *like* or *as* used to compare?   ○ yes   ○ no

❸ Are the words *like a bump on a log* part of a simile in this selection?   ○ yes ○ no

---

Name _____ Date _____

Simile ▶ **as hungry as a bear**

Meaning ▶ very hungry; someone who eats a lot of food or eats often

How It Is Used ▶ Mom commented on how fast my baby brother was growing. She told her friend, "My other two babies ate during regular meal times, and never ate more than six ounces at one feeding. This one is *as hungry as a bear*. He eats every two hours, and is already up to eight-ounce bottles."

Recognizing Similes ▶ **Remember: A simile is a comparison using *like* or *as*.**

Read the selection. Answer the questions below.

On a recent trip to a state park, the park ranger gave a talk about the wildlife in the area. People wondered how to protect their food while camping. "You have to worry about raccoons, because they are sneaky, but a raccoon wouldn't usually be *as hungry as a bear* might be."

❶ Is something being compared to something else?   ○ yes   ○ no

❷ Is the word *like* or *as* used to compare?   ○ yes   ○ no

❸ Are the words *as hungry as a bear* part of a simile in this selection?   ○ yes   ○ no

---

Simile ▶ **eats like a horse**

Meaning ▶ eats a lot of food; is constantly eating

How It Is Used ▶ My mom likes my friend Robby. But one thing about him bothers her. Whenever he comes over, he heads right for the refrigerator. "Robby is a nice boy," she said, "but he *eats like a horse*."

Recognizing Similes ▶ **Remember: A simile is a comparison using *like* or *as*.**

Read the selection. Answer the questions below.

After a fun day at the beach, we were all ready for a hamburger and chips. My Aunt Sarah always brought a huge watermelon to share with the family. My older brother ran to the picnic table. "Good thing there's lots of food," he said. "I'm so hungry, *I could eat a horse*."

❶ Is something being compared to something else?   ○ yes   ○ no

❷ Is the word *like* or *as* used to compare?   ○ yes   ○ no

❸ Are the words *eats like a horse* part of a simile in this selection?   ○ yes   ○ no

Name _____ Date _____

Simile ▶	**as strong as an ox**
Meaning ▶	very strong; with much force and strength
How It Is Used ▶	We watched as the movers picked up our heaviest furniture and carefully loaded it onto the moving vans. That man is as *strong as an ox,*" my dad commented.

Recognizing Similes ▶   **Remember: A simile is a comparison using *like* or *as*.**

Read the selection. Answer the questions below.

The museum had a special exhibit on ancient Egyptians. The audio tour explained how they moved heavy loads to build the pyramids. "Even with the equipment and help, they must have been as *strong as an ox* to build those massive structures," my friend whispered to me.

❶ Is something being compared to something else?   ◯ yes   ◯ no

❷ Is the word *like* or *as* used to compare?   ◯ yes   ◯ no

❸ Are the words as *strong as an ox* part of a simile in this selection?   ◯ yes   ◯ no

---

Simile ▶	**as sweet as honey**
Meaning ▶	very kind and thoughtful; extremely nice and caring
How It Is Used ▶	My friend Rachel and I were hoping we would get Mrs. Cash as our fifth grade teacher. Everyone knew she was the nicest teacher at our school. When school started, we were excited to see both our names on the list outside her door. When I told my mom when I got home, she said, "Mrs. Cash is as *sweet as honey*. You girls are going to have a great fifth grade year."

Recognizing Similes ▶   **Remember: A simile is a comparison using *like* or *as*.**

Read the selection. Answer the questions below.

In making the cake, we found that we didn't have any honey to spread on top. We looked in the cupboard for something as *sweet as honey* to use instead.

❶ Is something being compared to something else?   ◯ yes   ◯ no

❷ Is the word *like* or *as* used to compare?   ◯ yes   ◯ no

❸ Are the words as *sweet as honey* part of a simile in this selection?   ◯ yes   ◯ no

---

Name _____ Date _____

Simile ▶ **eat like a bird**

Meaning ▶ eat very little; eat slightly

How It Is Used ▶ My older sister gave us good advice before we rode the big rollercoaster. "If I were you, I would *eat like a bird* before going on that ride," she suggested. "A full stomach and rolling through loops and curves at 60 miles per hour just don't mix."

Recognizing Similes ▶ **Remember: A simile is a comparison using *like* or *as*.**
Read the selection. Answer the questions below.

Every morning, we would let our cat in from his night on the prowl. He was quite the hunter, so we were never sure what little surprise he would leave for us on our doorstep. Sometimes he would *eat a bird*. Another time, he left us a lizard. Once he even brought home a mole.

❶ Is something being compared to something else? ◯ yes ◯ no

❷ Is the word *like* or *as* used to compare? ◯ yes ◯ no

❸ Are the words *eat like a bird* part of a simile in this selection? ◯ yes ◯ no

---

Simile ▶ **feel/look like a million bucks**

Meaning ▶ feel great; feel like a person can do anything

How It Is Used ▶ Jenna looked nice every day for school. On picture day, she took great care with every detail of her clothes and hair. When she walked into the classroom in her red dress, Marcie told her, "Jenna, you *look like a million bucks* today!"

Recognizing Similes ▶ **Remember: A simile is a comparison using *like* or *as*.**
Read the selection. Answer the questions below.

Kylie was thrilled to learn that she had won a makeover at the area's best salon. However, she was nervous about what the stylist was going to do. "Don't you worry," he assured Kylie. "You will walk out of here in two hours *looking like a million bucks*."

❶ Is something being compared to something else? ◯ yes ◯ no

❷ Is the word *like* or *as* used to compare? ◯ yes ◯ no

❸ Are the words *feeling like a million bucks* part of a simile above? ◯ yes ◯ no

Name _____ Date _____

Simile ▶ **like the icing on the cake**

Meaning ▶ the extra thing that makes something else extra special; something that makes something good even better

How It Is Used ▶ Frank was looking forward to the camping trip with his Boy Scout troop. When he got there, he saw another troop camping in the same area. Then he realized his best friend from the other side of town was in that troop. When the two boys met up, Frank thought, "This is *like the icing on the cake*, having my best friend along on my camping trip!"

Recognizing Similes ▶ **Remember: A simile is a comparison using *like* or *as*.**

Read the selection. Answer the questions below.

At the birthday party, we all waited for the cake to be cut. Allison ate the cake but didn't *like the icing on the cake*.

❶ Is something being compared to something else?　　○ yes　　○ no

❷ Is the word *like* or *as* used to compare?　　○ yes　　○ no

❸ Are the words *like the icing on the cake* part of a simile above?　○ yes　○ no

---

Simile ▶ **as stubborn as a mule**

Meaning ▶ a person who will not change his or her mind or opinion, even if he or she is wrong

How It Is Used ▶ Mom knew Dad didn't like to fly. We wanted to go to Hawaii for our vacation, but Dad wouldn't change his mind. Mom said he was as *stubborn as a mule*.

Recognizing Similes ▶ **Remember: A simile is a comparison using *like* or *as*.**

Read the selection. Answer the questions below.

During my summer job on a farm, I got to know the animals pretty well. One day my little sister visited me. I pointed out the pigs and chickens, but she was more interested in the corral with the horses. "Just ignore that *stubborn mule*," I told her. "He thinks he is a horse."

❶ Is something being compared to something else?　　○ yes　　○ no

❷ Is the word *like* or *as* used to compare?　　○ yes　　○ no

❸ Are the words *as stubborn as a mule* part of a simile above?　○ yes　○ no

---

Expressions That Are Metaphors

This unit highlights idioms that are metaphors. Below are two lists of metaphors. The first, *Ten to Teach*, presents the 10 metaphors introduced and taught in this unit. The second, *More to Mention*, offers additional expressions that you may want to mention or use to create additional activities.

Ten to Teach

1. top dog
2. make a beeline
3. eager beaver
4. round up (everyone)

5. chew on (something)
6. puff up
7. buy into it
8. keep your paws off

9. time stood still
10. caught one's breath

More to Mention

▶ all pumped up*
▶ scaredy-cat*
▶ statue*
▶ all bark and no bite*
▶ hollow voice*

▶ see the writing on the wall
▶ steamed up
▶ left holding the bag
▶ take forty winks
▶ at the end of one's rope

▶ stretch the point
▶ break the silence
▶ hit a snag
▶ hard to swallow
▶ on the edge of one's seat

These metaphors are also included in the story but are not highlighted individually in the unit.

Using This Unit

Begin by reading the basic *Ten to Teach* metaphors. Ask the students if they have ever heard or used any of these expressions, and if so, how and where. Next, read them again, and this time ask the students to listen for what they have in common. The students should see that the expressions compare one thing to another. Teach or review the definition of a *metaphor*—a direct comparison. Explain that a metaphor is like a simile, without using *like* or *as* to compare. You can read the list again and let the students identify the comparison in each metaphor.

On the next page is a story that includes the *Ten to Teach* metaphors (along with five *More to Mention* metaphors). Note that the story is not intended to be an example of good writing; it would not be natural to use 15 metaphors in such a short piece. The purpose of the story is simply to use all the expressions in context. The story is at approximately a 4.2 reading level. Use this information to read it aloud to students, have them read it, or both. This reproducible page includes the story and questions for students to answer.

The final five pages of the unit introduce the basic *Ten to Teach* metaphors individually, two to a page. These can be reproduced and used as is, or cut apart into separate cards. Use these after the story to reinforce the meanings of the metaphors or test students' understanding of them. Or, use them before the story as preparation for reading or for scaffolding as needed.

Note: As in the previous unit on similes, in this unit students are asked questions that lead them to decide if a phrase in a selection is used as a metaphor or not.

Optional: Use one of the ideas or activities in the introductory section of this book as an extension or follow-up to the unit.

Name _____ Date _____

Below is a story that includes 15 metaphors. Can you tell what they mean?

The Secret of the Trap Door

Of the five members of the Olive Street Detectives Club, Jason was the **top dog**. So, when Marissa discovered a secret trap door in the ground in the field right behind the neighborhood, she **made a beeline** straight to Jason's. "Let's go open it!" she said, **all pumped up**.

"Don't be such an **eager beaver**," Jason answered. "We'll **round up everyone** for a meeting to **chew on** the best way to investigate."

Although the other kids thought Jason was fearless, deep down he was a **scaredy-cat**. He just **puffed himself up** in front of the others and they **bought into it**. Until now, they hadn't ever actually found anything.

When the whole group assembled at the wooden door in the field, Daniel started tugging at the door. "Hey! **Keep your paws off** that!" barked Jason. However, it was too late. The door popped open. **Time stood still** for a moment, and when the kids **caught their breath**, Daniel said, "It's like a tunnel," and disappeared into the hole in the ground.

Meg turned to Jason. "What should we do?" But Jason was a **statue**, too stunned to reply. The group's fearless leader revealed that he was **all bark and no bite**.

No one spoke for a moment or two. Then, from somewhere deep in ground came Daniel's **hollow voice**. "Hey, guys," it echoed up to them. "Someone lives down here!"

"Or some*thing* . . . ." whispered Marissa.

Read or listen to the story again. Then answer these questions about the metaphors. To help you find them, the metaphors are in **dark print** in the story.

1. Who was the leader of the Olive Street Detectives Club at the beginning of the story?

   _____

2. What was Jason's secret? How was it revealed?

   _____

3. How did the kids react to the opening of the trap door?

   _____

4. Do you think Jason will continue to be the club's leader? Explain your answer.

   _____

Name _____ Date _____

Metaphor ▶ **top dog**

Meaning ▶ the person in charge; the person who is the best at something

How It Is Used ▶ My dad was hoping to get a big promotion last week. But when his boss came into his office, the news wasn't what my dad had expected. "We hired Jack Newsom for the opening," his boss said. "He was the *top dog* at our biggest competitor."

Recognizing Metaphors ▶ **Remember: A metaphor is a direct comparison (without the words *like* or *as*).**

Read the selection. Answer the questions below.

Gina was in charge of the poodle circus act. Today they were working on building a dog pyramid. The largest dogs were on the bottom. The smallest and lightest poodle was the *top dog*.

❶ Is something being compared to something else?   ○ yes   ○ no

❷ Is the word *like* or *as* used to compare?   ○ yes   ○ no

❸ Are the words *top dog* part of a metaphor in this example?   ○ yes   ○ no

---

Metaphor ▶ **make a beeline**

Meaning ▶ quickly move directly toward something; go somewhere without stopping

How It Is Used ▶ It was the hottest week of the summer, so Mom offered to take us to the beach. I don't think our car was even in park before my friends and I *made a beeline* for the water.

Recognizing Metaphors ▶ **Remember: A metaphor is a direct comparison (without the words *like* or *as*).**

Read the selection. Answer the questions below.

After a long walk, our elderly neighbor likes to sit and rest on her porch. The minute her dog, Felix, gets in the door, he *makes a beeline* for his water bowl.

❶ Is something being compared to something else?   ○ yes   ○ no

❷ Is the word *like* or *as* used to compare?   ○ yes   ○ no

❸ Are the words *make a beeline* part of a metaphor in this example?   ○ yes   ○ no

---

Name _____ Date _____

Metaphor ▶ **eager beaver**

Meaning ▶ hard worker; someone who is ready and willing to do just about anything

How It Is Used ▶ Jared and Rudy had a whole month to complete their history project. Jared thought they could meet in a couple of weeks at the library. But Rudy was an *eager beaver* and suggested they start at his house this Saturday.

Recognizing Metaphors ▶ **Remember: A metaphor is a direct comparison (without the words *like* or *as*).**

Read the selection. Answer the questions below.

On our hike, we came across a family of beavers. Some were swimming, some were resting, and others were playing. But one *eager beaver* was busily building a dam.

❶ Is something being compared to something else? ○ yes ○ no

❷ Is the word *like* or *as* used to compare? ○ yes ○ no

❸ Are the words *eager beaver* part of a metaphor in this example? ○ yes ○ no

---

Metaphor ▶ **round up (everyone)**

Meaning ▶ call or gather people, animals, or things together in one place

How It Is Used ▶ The delicious aroma of Grandma's lasagna led people right to the kitchen. When dinner was ready to serve, she didn't have to work very hard to *round everyone up*.

Recognizing Metaphors ▶ **Remember: A metaphor is a direct comparison (without the words *like* or *as*).**

Read the selection. Answer the questions below.

To round up numbers to the nearest ten, use the digit in the ones place. If the digit is 0, 1, 2, 3, or 4, the digit in the tens column stays the same, and a 0 is placed in the ones column. If the digit is 5, 6, 7, 8, or 9, *round up* the digit in the tens column to the next number, and place a 0 in the ones column.

❶ Is something being compared to something else? ○ yes ○ no

❷ Is the word *like* or *as* used to compare? ○ yes ○ no

❸ Are the words *round up* part of a metaphor in this example? ○ yes ○ no

Expressions That Are Metaphors *(cont.)*

Name _____ Date _____

Metaphor ▶ **chew on (something)**

Meaning ▶ think over; think about; consider for a while

How It Is Used ▶ When Dad emerged from Bobby's room, Mom asked about Bobby's punishment for coming in past curfew. "We talked for a while, and I let him *chew on* some possible punishments. He has until Sunday to choose."

Recognizing Metaphors ▶ **Remember: A metaphor is a direct comparison (without the words *like* or *as*).**

Read the selection. Answer the questions below.

Roger wanted to try a gum experiment. He bought bubble gum that he could *chew on* for a long time. He blew bubbles first with one piece, then with two pieces. He believed the bubbles blown with two pieces would be twice the size of those blown with one piece.

❶ Is something being compared to something else? ⃝ yes ⃝ no

❷ Is the word *like* or *as* used to compare? ⃝ yes ⃝ no

❸ Are the words *chew on* part of a metaphor in this example? ⃝ yes ⃝ no

---

Metaphor ▶ **puff up**

Meaning ▶ make something seem better than it really is; exaggerate

How It Is Used ▶ Mr. and Mrs. Carl knew that their babysitter, Sue, had had some bad nights in the past with their son, Jacob. Sue almost didn't agree to babysit. But Mrs. Carl *puffed up* Jacob's recent behavior so well that Sue agreed to try again.

Recognizing Metaphors ▶ **Remember: A metaphor is a direct comparison (without the words *like* or *as*).**

Read the selection. Answer the questions below.

Kerry really wanted a pet turtle. She did everything to *puff up* her story about their perfection as pets. After weeks of begging, Kerry's mom finally took her to the pet store.

❶ Is something being compared to something else? ⃝ yes ⃝ no

❷ Is the word *like* or *as* used to compare? ⃝ yes ⃝ no

❸ Are the words *puffed up* part of a metaphor in this example? ⃝ yes ⃝ no

---

Expressions That Are Metaphors (cont.)

Name _____   Date _____

Metaphor ▶ **buy into it**

Meaning ▶ believe; agree; go along with an idea

How It Is Used ▶ The whole family wanted to get an action adventure movie for our regular Saturday night family movie night. My little sister, Haley, was the hardest to persuade. We told her about the excitement and star cast, but she wouldn't *buy into it*. We wound up with a family film instead.

Recognizing Metaphors ▶ **Remember: A metaphor is a direct comparison (without the words *like* or *as*).**

Read the selection. Answer the questions below.

Ned had heard that the haunted house at the carnival was incredible! He couldn't wait to see it. When they got there, Ned did all he could to reassure his sister that she wouldn't be too scared, but she wouldn't *buy into it*. She stood outside waiting for him while Ned went in alone.

❶ Is something being compared to something else?   ◯ yes   ◯ no

❷ Is the word *like* or *as* used to compare?   ◯ yes   ◯ no

❸ Are the words *buy into it* part of a metaphor in this example?   ◯ yes   ◯ no

---

Metaphor ▶ **keep your paws off**

Meaning ▶ leave something alone; don't touch or bother

How It Is Used ▶ Terry was very proud of his new pet gecko, King. Terry had only one worry: his little brother Greg. Terry sternly warned Greg to keep his distance. "*Keep* your body out of my room, and *your paws off* King!"

Recognizing Metaphors ▶ **Remember: A metaphor is a direct comparison (without the words *like* or *as*).**

Read the selection. Answer the questions below.

Betty was furious with her dog, Maverick. She had come home from school to find her favorite shoes chewed up and her bedspread muddy. Maverick tried to look innocent, but he had left signs of his handiwork. While cleaning up the mess, Betty continued to yell at her dog. "I told you to *keep your paws off* my bed!"

❶ Is something being compared to something else?   ◯ yes   ◯ no

❷ Is the word *like* or *as* used to compare?   ◯ yes   ◯ no

❸ Are the words *keep your paws off* part of a metaphor above?   ◯ yes   ◯ no

---

Name _____ Date _____

Metaphor ▶ **time stood still**

Meaning ▶ a brief moment when nothing seems to happen; usually follows a shocking event

How It Is Used ▶ Hannah had never before heard the sound of the ocean, so *time stood still* when she first visited a tropical island.

Recognizing Metaphors ▶ **Remember: A metaphor is a direct comparison (without the words *like* or *as*).**

Read the selection. Answer the questions below.

Michelle was always in trouble when her report card came home. But last week, Michelle surprised her parents with two *A*s and three *B*s. When her parents opened her report card, it seemed like *time stood still*. Then they smiled and hugged Michelle for doing so much better.

❶ Is something being compared to something else?   ○ yes   ○ no

❷ Is the word *like* or *as* used to compare?   ○ yes   ○ no

❸ Are the words *time stood still* part of a metaphor in this example?   ○ yes   ○ no

---

Metaphor ▶ **caught one's breath**

Meaning ▶ recovered from a shocking or scary event; taking a break from hard work

How It Is Used ▶ Jamey was about to step onto the canoe when it moved away from the dock. She *caught her breath* as her dad grabbed her arm, keeping her from falling off the dock.

Recognizing Metaphors ▶ **Remember: A metaphor is a direct comparison (without the words *like* or *as*).**

Read the selection. Answer the questions below.

As the announcer approached the microphone, we eagerly awaited to hear whether our school won the state academic challenge. When he said, "The winner is Meadows Elementary School," our principal had to *catch her breath*.

❶ Is something being compared to something else?   ○ yes   ○ no

❷ Is the word *like* or *as* used to compare?   ○ yes   ○ no

❸ Are the words *catch her breath* part of a metaphor in this example?   ○ yes   ○ no

Expressions That Exaggerate (Hyperbole)

This unit highlights expressions that exaggerate (hyperbole). Below are two lists of expressions. The first, *Ten to Teach*, presents the 10 expressions introduced and taught in this unit. The second, *More to Mention*, offers additional examples in this theme that you may want to mention or use to create additional activities.

Ten to Teach

1. go through the roof
2. head over heels
3. knee-high to a grasshopper
4. cost an arm and a leg
5. until the cows come home

6. born yesterday
7. highway robbery
8. everything but the kitchen sink
9. find a needle in a haystack
10. made of money

More to Mention

▶ wild horses couldn't drag me away*
▶ on top of the world*
▶ when pigs fly*
▶ burns me up*
▶ ton of money*

▶ on one's last leg
▶ over my dead body
▶ the sky's the limit
▶ bursting at the seams
▶ turn over in one's grave

▶ cry a river*
▶ chilled to the bone
▶ die of boredom
▶ full of hot air
▶ the last straw

These expressions are also included in the story but are not highlighted individually in the unit.

Using This Unit

Read to students the basic *Ten to Teach* expressions. Ask them if they have ever heard or used these expressions. Next, reread the expressions, and ask the students to listen for what they have in common. Accept all answers, and then point out that all the expressions exaggerate, or say something that could never be true as described. Tell students that this is called *hyperbole*.

On the next page is a story that includes the *Ten to Teach* expressions (along with six *More to Mention* expressions). Note that the story is not intended to be an example of good writing; it would not be natural to use 16 exaggerations in such a short piece. The purpose of the story is simply to use all the expressions in context. The story is at approximately a 4.8 reading level. Use this information to read it aloud to students, have them read it, or both. This reproducible page includes the story and questions for students.

The final five pages of the unit introduce the basic *Ten to Teach* expressions individually, two to a page. These can be reproduced and used as is or cut into separate cards. Use these after the story to reinforce the meanings of these expressions, or use them before the story as preparation.

Note: As in the previous unit on metaphors, students are asked questions that lead them to decide whether or not a phrase in a selection is used as an exaggeration.

Optional: Use one of the ideas or activities in the introductory section of this book as an extension or follow-up to the unit.

Expressions That Exaggerate (Hyperbole) *(cont.)*

Name _____ Date _____

Below is a story containing 16 expressions that exaggerate. Can you tell what they mean?

Sports Dilemma

I want to talk about a subject that just makes me **go through the roof**. Here's the deal: I love to watch football. **Wild horses couldn't drag me away** from the TV on game day. I go **head over heels** for my favorite team. When they win, I am **on top of the world**. When they lose, I feel like I could **cry a river** of tears. Even though I am only **knee-high to a grasshopper** next to the big offensive lineman and tall receivers, I am their biggest fan.

A couple of things really bother me, though. First, I would like to wear my team's logo shirt during the games and even buy some of the team merchandise, but everything **costs an arm and a leg**! Even if I saved my allowance **until the cows came home**, I couldn't afford to buy even one shirt. Would my parents buy it for me? **When pigs fly**! I wasn't **born yesterday**. I know to not even ask.

Besides the cost being **highway robbery**, there's another problem. There is official team merchandise for sale that includes **everything but the kitchen sink**—hats, sweatshirts, mugs, little bobblehead figures, plaques, towels, and even socks and underwear. However, with all this stuff available to buy, it is like **finding a needle in a haystack** to come up with anything that is made for girls. Oh, didn't I mention that I'm a girl? You probably assumed that I was a boy, just like the people who make and market team shirts and other merchandise. This really **burns me up**! Why do the football team owners assume that their fans are all men and boys? Look at the people in the stands sometime. There are a lot of women and girls at the games! Why don't we count? Where are my team socks and T-shirt?

So I want to send a message to the people who make team merchandise. First, make some stuff for girls—just for girls—like team hair accessories or earrings with our teams' logos! Second, offer at least a few things that people who aren't **made of money** could afford. In the long run, you would still make a **ton of money** because you would sell more to more people. How about it?

Read or listen to the story again. Then answer these questions about the expressions. To help you find them, the exaggerations are in **dark print** in the story.

1. What is the author upset about? _____

2. How does the author feel about her favorite team? _____

3. What is the problem with team merchandise? _____

4. Why did the author write this passage? _____

5. If you were in charge of team merchandise, what changes would you make?

   _____

Name _____ Date _____

Hyperbole ▶ **go through the roof**

Meaning ▶ get very angry; increase quickly or go very high (such as price)

How It Is Used ▶ My mom found information about summer sailing camp. When she learned the price, she *went through the roof*!

Recognizing Hyperbole ▶ **Remember: Hyperbole is an expression that exaggerates, or describes something as greatly more or less than it really is, and could not actually be true.**

Read the selection. Answer the questions below.

We huddled together in the bathroom to wait out the storm. Just when we thought the storm was dying down, we heard a loud crash. When we emerged from the bathroom, we saw that a tree had *gone through the roof.*

❶ What does the phrase *gone through the roof* here describe? ○ price or cost ○ tree

❷ Is something described in a way that could not actually be true? ○ yes ○ no

❸ Does the description use hyperbole? ○ yes ○ no

Hyperbole ▶ **head over heels**

Meaning ▶ very excited (feeling like you want to do flips); in love

How It Is Used ▶ Grace wanted a new puppy. Her mom took her to the animal shelter where she could find one she liked. As soon as she saw the sweet cocker spaniel staring up at her with its big, brown eyes, Grace fell *head over heels*.

Recognizing Hyperbole ▶ **Remember: Hyperbole is an expression that exaggerates, or describes something as greatly more or less than it really is, and could not actually be true.**

Read the selection. Answer the questions below.

I complained to my mom that my friend Sherry only wanted to talk about this one actor in a new movie. "Don't worry," my mom assured me. "Sherry is *head over heels* for him right now. Eventually, she will lose interest, and you girls can go back to talking about other things."

❶ What does the phrase *head over heels* here describe? ○ a new movie ○ Sherry's feelings

❷ Is something described in a way that could not actually be true? ○ yes ○ no

❸ Does the description use hyperbole? ○ yes ○ no

Name _____ Date _____

Hyperbole ▶ knee–high to a grasshopper

Meaning ▶ small and young; not old

How It Is Used ▶ Carol looked forward to revisiting the house where she was born. "Nothing looks familiar," Carol remarked upon their arrival. "Well, I guess it wouldn't," her mom explained. "The last time we were here, you were just *knee-high to a grasshopper.*"

Recognizing Hyperbole ▶ Remember: Hyperbole is an expression that exaggerates, or describes something as greatly more or less than it really is, and could not actually be true.

Read the selection. Answer the questions below.

We were meeting my cousin, Jasper, at the airport. It had been years since we had seen him. My mom almost didn't recognize him when he got off the plane. "The last time I saw you, Jasper," my mom said, "you were *knee-high to a grasshopper.*"

❶ What does the phrase *knee-high to a grasshopper* here describe?

○ Jasper as a boy ○ a grasshopper

❷ Is something described in a way that could not actually be true? ○ yes ○ no

❸ Does the description use hyperbole? ○ yes ○ no

Hyperbole ▶ cost an arm and a leg

Meaning ▶ cost a lot of money; expensive

How It Is Used ▶ Pete begged his mom and dad to get one of the newest televisions on the market. It had the clearest picture and sound, and it could be hooked up to create an incredible home theater system. "Not just now," Pete's dad replied. "Right now, those TV sets *cost an arm and a leg.* We'll wait a few years until the price comes down."

Recognizing Hyperbole ▶ Remember: Hyperbole is an expression that exaggerates, or describes something as greatly more or less than it really is, and could not actually be true.

Read the selection. Answer the questions below.

While basking in the sun, Mr. Gordon reflected on how much his family was enjoying their first cruise. "This sure *cost me an arm and a leg,*" he said. "But it is an adventure our family will remember for a long time to come."

❶ What does the phrase *cost me an arm and a leg* here describe? ○ cruise ○ body parts

❷ Is something described in a way that could not actually be true? ○ yes ○ no

❸ Does the description use hyperbole? ○ yes ○ no

Name _____ Date _____

Hyperbole ▶ **until the cows come home**

Meaning ▶ a very long time in the future; for a long time

How It Is Used ▶ The inflatable pool was too difficult for my little brother to blow up. He could have blown *until the cows came home*, but he never would have fully inflated it.

Recognizing Hyperbole ▶ **Remember: Hyperbole is an expression that exaggerates, or describes something as greatly more or less than it really is, and could not actually be true.**

Read the selection. Answer the questions below.

Working at the ranch all summer was harder work than Oscar thought. Dinner wasn't served *until the cows came home* and all the other animals were rounded up.

❶ What does the phrase *until the cows came home* here describe? ○ dinner ○ cows

❷ Is something described in a way that could not actually be true? ○ yes ○ no

❸ Does the description use hyperbole? ○ yes ○ no

Hyperbole ▶ **born yesterday**

Meaning ▶ not smart; not knowing very much

How It Is Used ▶ The neighbors set up their haunted house for Halloween. When their son, Billy, tried to convince me that it was really haunted, I just laughed. "He must think I was *born yesterday*," I thought.

Recognizing Hyperbole ▶ **Remember: Hyperbole is an expression that exaggerates, or describes something as greatly more or less than it really is, and could not actually be true.**

Read the selection. Answer the questions below.

Matilda was upset that her mother did not tell her that her aunt's cats had kittens. "Oh, Matilda, I just forgot," her mother explained. "Besides, they were just *born yesterday*."

❶ What does the phrase *born yesterday* here describe? ○ Matilda ○ kittens

❷ Is something described in a way that could not actually be true? ○ yes ○ no

❸ Does the description use hyperbole? ○ yes ○ no

Name _____ Date _____

Hyperbole ▶	**highway robbery**
Meaning ▶	charging way too much for something; too costly
How It Is Used ▶	When a pipe broke in his home, Mr. Blake called a plumber right away. "Those weekend plumbers get away with *highway robbery*," Mr. Blake complained after he had paid the bill.
Recognizing Hyperbole ▶	**Remember: Hyperbole is an expression that exaggerates, or describes something as greatly more or less than it really is, and could not actually be true.**

Read the selection. Answer the questions below.

Wanda and her friends enjoyed going to the movies on the weekend. The one thing they didn't like, however, was how much popcorn, candy, and drinks cost. Last time, they paid more for snacks than they did for their tickets! "That's *highway robbery*," Wanda mumbled as she paid.

❶ What does the phrase *highway robbery* here describe? ○ the cost of the food and drink
○ the highway

❷ Is something described in a way that could not actually be true? ○ yes ○ no

❸ Does the description use hyperbole? ○ yes ○ no

Hyperbole ▶	**everything but the kitchen sink**
Meaning ▶	lots of things; more things than is necessary
How It Is Used ▶	The salesperson really talked up the stereo system Bill was admiring. "Yes, this baby has *everything but the kitchen sink*," she said. "Besides all the regular features, it has a timer and an automatic station scanner."
Recognizing Hyperbole ▶	**Remember: Hyperbole is an expression that exaggerates, or describes something as greatly more or less than it really is, and could not actually be true.**

Read the selection. Answer the questions below.

The builder was walking through Mrs. Morgan's new house with her. "I hope everything is OK," he said. "*Everything but the kitchen sink* has been installed. That will be delivered next week."

❶ What does the phrase *everything but the kitchen sink* here describe? ○ the house
○ the kitchen sink

❷ Is something described in a way that could not actually be true? ○ yes ○ no

❸ Does the description use hyperbole? ○ yes ○ no

Name _____ Date _____

Hyperbole ▶ **find a needle in a haystack**

Meaning ▶ look for something that a person will probably never find

How It Is Used ▶ When Kim's bracelet burst, every last bead landed in the shag carpet. We got down on our hands and knees to help her find the beads. It was like trying to *find a needle in a haystack*.

Recognizing Hyperbole ▶ **Remember: Hyperbole is an expression that exaggerates, or describes something as greatly more or less than it really is, and could not actually be true.**

Read the selection. Answer the questions below.

The daycare workers set up a game in which the children dug in sand to find buried pennies. "This is like *finding a needle in a haystack*," said one worker. "They'll be digging for hours!"

❶ What does the phrase *finding a needle in a haystack* here describe?
○ digging for pennies   ○ a needle

❷ Is something described in a way that could not actually be true?   ○ yes   ○ no

❸ Does the description use hyperbole?   ○ yes   ○ no

Hyperbole ▶ **made of money**

Meaning ▶ having a lot of money; usually used to mean that a person doesn't have the money needed for something

How It Is Used ▶ Penny really wanted a car for her 16th birthday. Her parents didn't want to disappoint her, but they knew it cost too much. "You talk like we are *made of money*!" her mom exclaimed.

Recognizing Hyperbole ▶ **Remember: Hyperbole is an expression that exaggerates, or describes something as greatly more or less than it really is, and could not actually be true.**

Read the selection. Answer the questions below.

Aunt Sue liked to decorate her house with unusual artwork and trinkets. Over her fireplace is a picture entirely *made of money*. It is a mosaic of coins and bills.

❶ What does the phrase *made of money* here describe?   ○ picture   ○ money

❷ Is something described in a way that could not actually be true?   ○ yes   ○ no

❸ Does the description use hyperbole?   ○ yes   ○ no

Common Sayings (Proverbs)

This unit highlights expressions that are proverbs. *Proverbs* are common sayings that apply to a variety of situations. Below is a list of 20 expressions. All 20 proverbs are introduced and taught in this unit.

Twenty to Teach

1. That's easier said than done.
2. If the shoe fits, wear it.
3. Birds of a feather flock together.
4. Blood is thicker than water.
5. Don't look a gift horse in the mouth.
6. Be careful what you wish for.
7. A stitch in time saves nine.
8. You can't teach an old dog new tricks.
9. Don't put all your eggs in one basket.
10. Time flies when you're having fun.
11. Necessity is the mother of invention.
12. Let sleeping dogs lie.
13. Rome wasn't built in a day.
14. Haste makes waste.
15. Too many cooks spoil the broth.
16. Strike while the iron is hot.
17. Variety is the spice of life.
18. Cat got your tongue?
19. Two wrongs don't make a right.
20. No news is good news.

Using This Unit

Begin by reading to students the 20 proverbs. First ask students if they have ever heard or used any of these expressions, and if so, how and where. Next, explain to students that proverbs are common sayings. Like idioms, the words do not mean what they actually say. Rather, they express truth, advice, or wisdom about a variety of situations.

On the next two pages is a list of meanings for each of the 20 proverbs. Note that the meanings given may not be precise definitions. As the class reviews the definitions, have students offer their own interpretations of the proverbs. Use these reproducible pages to introduce and discuss each proverb. There is a place for students to mark which proverbs they have heard or used themselves. Students may keep this list in their writing folders as a reference during their independent writing time.

The final four pages of this special unit offer a series of vignettes. Each story could end with a proverb. On each page, five proverbs are suggested for three situational stories. Students read or listen to each situation, then choose the appropriate proverb that best fits at the end of the story. The directions instruct students to use the two proverbs not selected in their own situation on the back of the page. By completing all four pages, students will have analyzed each of the 20 proverbs, and will have used context clues to apply the correct one.

Optional: Use one of the ideas or activities in the introductory section of this book as an extension or follow-up to the unit.

Name _____ Date _____

Below are some expressions called *proverbs*. Proverbs are common sayings. Like idioms, the words do not actually mean what they say. They express truth, advice, or wisdom about a variety of situations. Read each of the 20 proverbs and their meanings. Put a ✓ by the ones that you have heard or used yourself. Be ready to describe a situation in which you heard or used it.

Proverb ▶ _____ That's easier said than done.

Meaning ▶ Something that sounds simple but could be really difficult

Proverb ▶ _____ If the shoe fits, wear it.

Meaning ▶ Telling someone to accept something as it is

Proverb ▶ _____ Birds of a feather flock together.

Meaning ▶ People who are alike tend to stay with one another.

Proverb ▶ _____ Blood is thicker than water.

Meaning ▶ Family is more important than anything.

Proverb ▶ _____ Don't look a gift horse in the mouth.

Meaning ▶ Telling someone not to complain when they get something for free.

Proverb ▶ _____ Be careful what you wish for.

Meaning ▶ Sometimes something a person thinks he or she wants really turns out to be not such a great thing.

Proverb ▶ _____ A stitch in time saves nine.

Meaning ▶ Be careful and take your time. If a person goes too fast, he or she may make a mistake and have to start over.

Proverb ▶ _____ You can't teach an old dog new tricks.

Meaning ▶ Once someone has a certain way of doing something, he or she does not change easily.

Proverb ▶ _____ Don't put all your eggs in one basket.

Meaning ▶ If a person counts on just one thing, he or she may miss other opportunities.

Proverb ▶ _____ Time flies when you're having fun.

Meaning ▶ When people are having fun, time seems to go by more quickly than usual.

Name _____ Date _____

Proverb ▶ _____ Necessity is the mother of invention.

Meaning ▶ When people really need something, they get creative and design or create it themselves.

Proverb ▶ _____ Let sleeping dogs lie.

Meaning ▶ Let something bad that happened in the past stay in the past, and don't bring it up again.

Proverb ▶ _____ Rome wasn't built in a day.

Meaning ▶ Some tasks take a long time to complete if they are to be done well.

Proverb ▶ _____ Haste makes waste.

Meaning ▶ Things done too quickly sometimes are not the best they could be had someone taken his or her time.

Proverb ▶ _____ Too many cooks spoil the broth.

Meaning ▶ When too many people are involved in something, it usually does not turn out well.

Proverb ▶ _____ Strike while the iron is hot.

Meaning ▶ Take advantage of the perfect time and the perfect place; don't let an opportunity pass by.

Proverb ▶ _____ Variety is the spice of life.

Meaning ▶ Change makes life worth living.

Proverb ▶ _____ Cat got your tongue?

Meaning ▶ Used when a person appears speechless; when a person is so shocked that he or she cannot talk.

Proverb ▶ _____ Two wrongs don't make a right.

Meaning ▶ When something bad happens, doing something bad to get back doesn't fix the situation.

Proverb ▶ _____ No news is good news.

Meaning ▶ A person can't receive bad news if there is no news; sometimes not knowing is better than knowing.

Common Sayings—Pick the Proverbs Part 1

Name _____ Date _____

Below are five proverbs. Remember, proverbs are common sayings. Like idioms, the words do not actually mean what they say; instead, they express truth, advice, or wisdom about situations. Read each story. Choose the proverb that would best fit at the end of the story. Write it on the line. Use the remaining two proverbs in your own story on the back of this page.

That's easier said than done.

Blood is thicker than water.

If the shoe fits, wear it.

Don't look a gift horse in the mouth.

Birds of a feather flock together.

Story 1

The Bellamy family had been upset over Uncle Frank being in trouble with the law. He had a hard time finding a job. He had little or no money to pay for food or rent. When he did go to look for work, he left his car parked in the wrong places. The parking tickets were piling up, but he could not pay for them.

Uncle Frank would be put in jail if he didn't pay his fines. Rather than let Uncle Frank be put behind bars, Mr. Bellamy told his brother he could stay with them for a few weeks and that he would pay Uncle Frank's parking tickets. He also offered to help him find a job.

Mrs. Bellamy was less than happy to have Frank stay with them. Mr. Bellamy reminded his wife that _____

Story 2

Gina had tried out for the volleyball team. She could serve well, and she had one mean spike. But Coach Wells knew that Gina liked to joke around. She had seen her in the halls playing pranks on her friends. In the lunchroom, Gina had once poured salt in someone's milk to get a good laugh. Coach Wells was not sure she wanted someone like that on the team.

When the coach made the final cuts, Gina was not on the team. When Gina went up to the coach to ask why she hadn't made the team, the coach told her that it was well-known that she was a prankster and that the volleyball team was no place for a class clown. She continued to complain, but the coach told her, "_____

Story 3

The Jacobs were on vacation during the holidays, and they had to take a plane and then rent a car to get to their hotel. But their flight was delayed and they got to the rental car counter late. The clerk told them there were no more cars available for rent.

"We'll just rent a car from another company," Mrs. Jacobs said. But the clerk told them that due to the holiday crowds, "_____

Common Sayings—Pick the Proverbs Part 2

Name _____ Date _____

Below are five proverbs. Remember, proverbs are common sayings. Like idioms, the words do not actually mean what they say; instead, they express truth, advice, or wisdom about situations. Read each story. Choose the proverb that would best fit at the end of the story. Write it on the line. Use the remaining two proverbs in your own story on the back of this page.

Be careful what you wish for.

Don't put all your eggs in one basket.

A stitch in time saves nine.

Time flies when you're having fun.

You can't teach an old dog new tricks.

Story 4

Ramon was lonely as the only child. He begged his mom and dad for a little brother or sister. After years of waiting, Ramon's family welcomed baby Maria into the family.

After Maria was born, Ramon had to make some changes. He couldn't play his video games when the baby was sleeping. He and his friends had to be careful that they weren't too noisy around the baby. And his mom expected him to help empty the diaper pail!

Ramon felt bad one day when his friend had to leave early because Maria had a doctor's appointment. His friend commented on his way out the door: "Let this be a lesson for you. You should _____

Story 5

Jan put posters out around her neighborhood. She offered to watch after dogs and cats while people were on vacation. Her mom suggested she post flyers in two other neighborhoods within walking distance, too.

"I don't want to go so far," Jan said to her mom.

"Well, the more you advertise, the more often you may be called," her mom advised. "By just advertising in our neighborhood, you are limiting your options. All I'm saying is, _____

_____

Story 6

Pablo liked teaching his grandma how to use the computer. He showed her how to open a program, and how to type and print a letter. He even showed her how she could use another program to manage her bank records.

In spite of Pablo's help, his grandmother was confused, and had a hard time with simple tasks.

"You're a good teacher, Pablo, but I know it will take me some time to get the hang of this," his grandma said. "It's true what they say, _____

Common Sayings—Pick the Proverbs Part 3

Name _____ Date _____

Below are five proverbs. Remember, proverbs are common sayings. Like idioms, the words do not actually mean what they say; instead, they express truth, advice, or wisdom about situations. Read each story. Choose the proverb that would best fit at the end of the story. Write it on the line. Use the remaining two proverbs in your own story on the back of this page.

Necessity is the mother of invention.   **Haste makes waste.**

Let sleeping dogs lie.   **Too many cooks spoil the broth.**

Rome wasn't built in a day.

Story 7

Carl enjoyed solving puzzles and building models. He got started right away on a new airplane model after he bought it. He had saved up for months for it!

After working three hours every day on the plane, Carl became impatient. He felt like he had worked so long, yet the plane wasn't even half finished.

His mom brought him some cookies and a power drink to keep up his energy. "You know, Carl," she assured, " _____

Story 8

Brenda was heartbroken when her best friend, Marcia, stopped talking to her. Marcia had become friends with someone else. Marcia's new friend didn't like Brenda so much. Brenda found other girls to spend time with after school, but she missed Marcia. They had a lot of great memories.

After a few months, Marcia spoke to Brenda during recess. Before too long, the two girls were inseparable once again. Brenda never asked Marcia what happened between her and the other girl. She thought it best to _____

Story 9

Don always wanted to be the first to complete any task. This was true in art class when they were painting or using clay. It was true in math class when they had timed quizzes. This was true in the lunchroom, too, when he wanted to finish ahead of everyone and go out for recess.

Don usually met his goal, but he was never really happy with the outcome. His art looked sloppy or unfinished. He always missed problems on the quizzes. And sometimes he ate so fast that his stomach hurt.

Don's teacher tried to get him to realize that there were things more important than being first. "If you slow down a little, you'll do better and you'll feel better," she told him. "You have learned that _____

Name _____ Date _____

Below are five proverbs. Remember, proverbs are common sayings. Like idioms, the words do not actually mean what they say; instead, they express truth, advice, or wisdom about situations. Read each story. Choose the proverb that would best fit at the end of the story. Write it on the line. Use the remaining two proverbs in your own story on the back of this page.

Strike while the iron is hot.   **Two wrongs don't make a right.**

Variety is the spice of life.   **No news is good news.**

Cat got your tongue?

Story 10

My brothers are always fighting. Long car trips are the worst. The two of them always argue about something. Just last week, on our way to our cousin's house, Marcus started crying. When my mom asked what happened, he said that Anthony pushed him. "Hey, you pushed me first!" cried Anthony. Mom scolded both of them, but told Anthony that _____

_____

Story 11

Adrienne was the best salesperson at the electronics store where she worked. She had a great smile that instantly made customers feel comfortable. She knew everything there was to know about the products they sold. As soon as a person showed interest in a product, she was an expert in closing the deal. Adrienne's motto was, " _____

_____

Story 12

Allie had applied to five of her top colleges several months ago. She raced home each day to check the mail for any letter from any of the schools, telling her whether she had been accepted or not. She was getting quite anxious for some response. She was sure she would hear something by the end of the week, but when Friday came, her mom informed her that there was still no word.

"Try to stay positive, Allie," her mom consoled. "Something will come soon. In the meantime, try to remember that _____

_____

Many of the answers will show an example of how the students might respond. For many of the questions there may be more than one correct answer.

Page 19
1. wonderful (the cat's meow)
2. take the bull by the horns
3. friendly
4. Answers will vary.
5. Answers will vary.

Page 20
straight from the horse's mouth: 2
the cat's meow: 1

Page 21
squirrel away: 1
monkey around: 2

Page 22
hoof it: 2
all bark and no bite: 1

Page 23
goose is cooked: 2
take the bull by the horns: 1

Page 24
play cat and mouse: 1
bark up the wrong tree: 2

Page 26
1. as soon as the parents left
2. on her hands and knees (on all fours)
3. She did not ever want to babysit again (wouldn't touch it with a ten-foot pole); after she got paid, she changed her mind.
4. Answers will vary.

Page 27
go fifty-fifty: 2
think twice: 2

Page 28
no two ways about it: 1
nickel and dime: 1

Page 29
put two and two together: 2
one step ahead: 2

Page 30
on all fours: 1
forty winks: 2

Page 31
put in one's two cents: 1
touch (it) with a ten-foot pole: 2

Page 33
1. poorly (got off on the wrong foot)
2. bad mood (nose out of joint; tongue-lashing)
3. Any of the following: fought tooth and nail not to laugh; told Bobby to cut it out; gave Bobby the cold shoulder. It didn't work.
4. No, because he didn't think the teacher would believe him, and he didn't have a leg to stand on.
5. Answers will vary.

Page 34
got off on the wrong foot: 1
nose out of joint: 2

Page 35
a tongue-lashing: 2
shake a leg: 2

Page 36
fight tooth and nail: 1
breathing down one's neck: 2

Page 37
the cold shoulder: 1
a pain in the neck: 1

Page 38
get out of hand: 1
didn't have a leg to stand on: 2

Page 40
1. Yes; she said she had a heart of gold.
2. She didn't want her granddaughter to feel bad (her heart was in the right place).
3. Any of the following: heavy heart, heartbroken
4. She was an important part (the core) of the family.
5. Answers will vary.

Page 41
with a heavy heart: 2
heart stood still: 2

Page 42
heart of gold: 1
from the heart: 2

Page 43
heart set on: 1
heart in right place: 1

Page 44
didn't have the heart: 1
heartbroken: 2

Page 45
heart and soul: 2
place in one's heart: 1

Page 47
1. bad
2. annoyed
3. no
4. Answers will vary.

Page 48
wake up on the wrong side of the bed: 2
rub someone the wrong way: 1

Page 49
on cloud nine: 2
down in the dumps: 1

Page 50
in the hot seat: 1
run into a brick wall: 2

Page 51
go out on a limb: 2
flip one's lid: 2

Page 52
for the birds: 1
bent out of shape: 2

Page 54
1. She got soaking wet in the rain (soaked to the bone).
2. a high fever (temperature was sky-high; burning up with fever)
3. She was confused (in a fog) OR she became upset and cried (misty-eyed; a flood of tears).
4. She would get in trouble (in hot water) and do poorly on the test.
5. Answers will vary.

Page 55
under the weather: 1
raining cats and dogs: 2

Page 56
soaked to the bone: 1
usual sunny self: 2

Page 57
like water off a duck's back: 2
in a fog: 1

Page 58
misty-eyed: 1
a flood of tears: 1

Answer Key (cont.)

Page 59
burning up: 2
in hot water: 2

Page 61
1. He went to bed early (hit the hay early).
2. He was angry (blew a fuse).
3. Brandon thought Margie was slow, but she turned out to be a fast runner.
4. No
5. Answers will vary.

Page 62
piece of cake: 1
hit the hay: 2

Page 63
in the driver's seat: 2
blow a fuse: 1

Page 64
the short end of the stick: 1
leave in the dust: 1

Page 65
hands down: 2
second fiddle: 2

Page 66
hats off: 2
in the bag: 1

Page 68
1. Tim: hog, horse, ox; Tom: bear, bird, mule
2. Answers will vary.
3. having more energy and being smarter
4. Answers will vary.

Page 69
as different as night and day: 1. Y; 2. Y; 3. Y
like a bump on a log: 1. Y; 2. Y; 3. Y

Page 70
as hungry as a bear: 1. Y; 2. Y; 3. N
eats like a horse: 1. N; 2. N; 3. N

Page 71
as strong as an ox: 1. Y; 2. Y; 3. Y
as sweet as honey: 1. Y; 2. Y; 3. N

Page 72
eat like a bird: 1. N; 2. N; 3. N
feel like a million bucks: 1. Y; 2. Y; 3. Y

Page 73
icing on the cake: 1. N; 2. N; 3. N
as stubborn as a mule: 1. N; 2. N; 3. N

Page 75
1. Jason
2. He was really afraid of the unknown (scaredy-cat).
3. They didn't move (time stood still; caught their breath).
4. Answers will vary.

Page 76
top dog: 1. N; 2. N; 3. N
make a beeline: 1. N; 2. N; 3. Y

Page 77
eager beaver: 1. N; 2. N; 3. N
round up: 1. N; 2. N; 3. N

Page 78
chew on (something): 1. N; 2. N; 3. N
puff up: 1. N; 2. N; 3. Y

Page 79
buy into it: 1. N; 2. N; 3. Y
keep your paws off: 1. N; 2. N; 3. N

Page 80
time stood still: 1. N; 2. N; 3. Y
caught one's breath: 1. N; 2. N; 3. Y

Page 82
1. She can't find affordable team merchandise, or team merchandise for girls.
2. She is crazy about them (head over heels).
3. It is too expensive (costs an arm and a leg).
4. She is hoping to persuade the makers of team merchandise to lower their prices and include more merchandise for girls.
5. Answers will vary.

Page 83
go through the roof: 1. tree; 2. N; 3. N
head over heels: 1. Sherry's feelings; 2. Y; 3. Y

Page 84
knee-high to a grasshopper: 1. Jasper as a boy; 2. Y; 3. Y
cost an arm and a leg: 1. cruise; 2. Y; 3. Y

Page 85
until the cows come home: 1. cows; 2. N; 3. N
born yesterday: 1. kittens; 2. N; 3. N

Page 86
highway robbery: 1. the cost of the food and drinks; 2. Y; 3. Y
everything but the kitchen sink: 1. the kitchen sink; 2. N; 3. N

Page 87
find a needle in a haystack: 1. digging for pennies; 2. Y; 3. Y
made of money: 1. picture; 2. N; 3. N

Page 91
Story #1: blood is thicker than water
Story #2: if the shoe fits, wear it
Story #3: that's easier said than done

Page 92
Story #4: be careful what you wish for
Story #5: don't put all your eggs in one basket
Story #6: you can't teach an old dog new tricks

Page 93
Story #7: Rome wasn't built in a day
Story #8: let sleeping dogs lie
Story #9: haste makes waste

Page 94
Story #10: two wrongs don't make a right
Story #11: strike while the iron is hot
Story #12: no news is good news

#50159—Idioms and Other English Expressions © Shell Education